LLC For Beginners

The Most Resourced Guide on How to Begin

(How to Successfully Start and Maintain a Limited Liability Company)

Zachary Adams

Published By **Daniel Kaplan**

Zachary Adams

LLC For Beginners: The Most Resourced Guide on How to Begin (How to Successfully Start and Maintain a Limited Liability Company)

ISBN 978-1-7750979-7-6

No part of this guidebook shall be reproduced in any form without permission in writing from the publisher except in the case of brief quotations embodied in critical articles or reviews.

Legal & Disclaimer

The information contained in this book is not designed to replace or take the place of any form of medicine or professional medical advice. The information in this book has been provided for educational & entertainment purposes only.

The information contained in this book has been compiled from sources deemed reliable, and it is accurate to the best of the Author's knowledge; however, the Author cannot guarantee its accuracy and validity and cannot be held liable for any errors or omissions. Changes are periodically made to this book. You must consult your doctor or get professional medical advice before using any of the suggested remedies, techniques, or information in this book.

Upon using the information contained in this book, you agree to hold harmless the Author from and against any damages, costs, and expenses, including any legal fees potentially resulting from the application of any of the information provided by this guide. This disclaimer applies to any damages or injury caused by the use and application, whether directly or indirectly, of any advice or information presented, whether for breach of contract, tort, negligence, personal injury, criminal intent, or under any other cause of action.

You agree to accept all risks of using the information presented inside this book. You need to consult a professional medical practitioner in order to ensure you are both able and healthy enough to participate in this program.

Table Of Contents

Chapter 1: Starting Your Llc

The Limited Liability Company, as instead of a sole proprietorship or a company, gives you an additional level of legal security. The majority of them stand out against their proprietors.

In order to file as an LLC, you must take more steps and documents that differ by the state. In order to send these documents to the state, you might be required to pay fees. Even though forming an LLC will take greater time and effort however, it offers greater protection and protection should you have accidents.

Establishment

A company, like an LLC needs documentation that outlines the different people's duties within the business. Companies are comprised of shareholders who control the business Directors who manage the company, as well as officers who oversee the day-to-day activities of the firm.

If you want to incorporate as a corporation Your company will typically require bylaws as well as the articles of incorporation. However the specific requirements differ by state. Corporate taxation is different from other businesses.

Corporations are by far the most complicated kind of business with regards to legal requirements however, they also provide the highest level of secure. If you are a multi-owner entity or are expecting an increase in your business, a company might be the right choice.

LLC as an Individual

One person who is a member of an LLC solely for themselves is called the Individual LLC. It's a hybrid company arrangement that has the characteristics of an organization and a sole proprietorship. As a corporate entity, its owners are protected by their personal assets; its debts do not affect the company's assets. Losses and profits are recorded on the sole proprietor's income declaration as they're in sole ownership.

Sole proprietorship refers to an entity that is run by and managed by one owner. If it's not an Limited Liability Company or Corporation that has a sole owner, it is a property that is unique to the owner.

The Rules of a Single Member LLC

In this situation the answer is "yes." An LLC with a single member which is taxed as sole proprietorship is run and controlled by one person. However, it cannot be a sole ownership.

State laws govern the usage and supervision of limited liability corporations. There's no standard rule because each state views LLCs differently.

One of the major benefits of having being an LLC is the fact that its owner does not have to personally bear obligations and debts of the company however, a single-member LLC is similar as a sole proprietorship the sense of structure for management as well as taxation.

It is possible to hire staff members to assist you when you're the sole owner of an LLC.

If you're sole proprietor of your business, you may employ employees to assist you run your business. However, if you employ employees to manage the day-today operation of your company it is your responsibility to following any relevant LLC law and regulations in all instances. Employees are not the owners (members) or members of your firm.

LLC Vs. Partnership

Article LLC refers to two kinds of businesses which include limited liability companies as well as partnerships. Although they're both legal structures, they differ with respect to personal accountability and management control procedures, as well as formal procedures and various other factors.

Association Against LLC; Differences and Similarities

The Limited Liability Company (LLC) is a very popular corporate entity which shares some features similar to other legal structures, such as partnerships. They're similar in the manner they came into existence and also their "pass-through" method of taxation However, they differ on the basis of features including participant liability.

What is an Association?

A company is a form of firm that is owned by several partners, who are all co-owners. In order to form a business at least two parties are required to sign a contract to establish the business and manage the business for the purpose of earning money.

Partners are responsible for managing the company and also the company's earnings and loss.

The income amount is based on the investment initially made by the proprietor of the business.

There are a variety of partnerships that differ in accordance with the business sector as well as the owner's desires.

The process of forming an LLC requires registering the business in the state it's located. It's an LLC. A majority of Limited Liability Companies operate under an operating agreement, which specifies the number of inquiries from members and the responses questions "what if?" questions. An LLC is an entity that has tax advantages of a sole proprietorship, but it does not have the advantages of personal responsibility which makes it a less effective form of an entity in a society.

Personal, Limited Liability Means

The owners of the company have divided their wealth from judgments against the firm.

The owners of personal property for example, such as cars or home, are not able to be impacted by creditors in the event that they are sued by a company or has a debt for which may put the business in danger of. In the event of an owner's illegal, unprofessional or reckless behavior can result in the termination of the responsibility protection.

With these distinct characteristics Many people believe that the LLC structure to be the optimal combination of a corporate and partnership. It's a hybrid corporation-individual business model.

Selecting a name for your business

Every State has a unique process to form an LLC however they all use the same basic guidelines

Pick a company name. The name of your LLC must satisfy the following criteria:

It should be distinct from other LLCs within the state you reside in. It should declare it to be an "LLC" / "Limited Company."

Do not use words that are considered to be illegal in your particular state for example "bank" or "insurance." If you are registering your business in your state, it will register your company's name. You won't need to register anything further.

It is essential that the Articles of Incorporation must be submitted to the Registrar of Companies. The "articles of organisation" are an essential document to establish the legality of the LLC and provides specific information like your company's address, members' names, as well as your address. A majority of states require you to make your filing with the Secretary of State. Some states may require you to submit your paperwork to an additional office such as for instance, the Department of Commerce & Consumer Affairs, State Corporation Commission, Division of Corporations and Commercial Code or Department of Consumer & Regulatory Affairs.

Create a contract for business. Most states do not require operating agreements. For multi-member LLCs, an operating contract is recommended as it organizes your LLC's financials and organisational structure and gives guidelines for an efficient running. The operating agreement typically contains the rights of members, obligations, loss and profit distribution, as well as percentage interest.

Registration of your LLC with the state

It is strongly recommended since it safeguards the owners and others shareholders from obligation and liabilities that come to the company. It is done by segregating the company's assets and liabilities from the assets and liabilities of its owners.

If the business is legally registered as a partnership or sole proprietorship owners personally are responsible for any legal expenses for the company. In other words, if the business is not able to cover the entire amount of legal expenses that are incurred, owners will be accountable to pay these bills using their personal assets.

Registration in different States

If you plan to establish your business across multiple states it is best to start with registering your business with a local Limited Liability Company in one of the states. The state in which you will be operating is that your primary office will be situated. After that, you are able to create a foreign LLC in the state where you're planning to do business. The process of establishing foreign LLCs is as easy as submitting your documents for the business to the state's Secretary of State's Office and then paying the filing fees.

Ideal for Small Businesses

If you are a small business, the formation of an LLC Limited Liability Company is an great choice. Because LLCs don't require the lengthy process of registration. There is a possibility of changing your business's structure to one of a corporation when the business develops. It is however advised to register with an LLC initially. for the moment as the benefits offered by LLCs are sufficient to start your company.

It is essential to select an agent registered with the state in which you'll work during the registration procedure. Many states require companies to employ a registered agent who will be responsible to maintain communication channels with relevant authorities. In order to sign and receive official documents, wage garnishments as well as tax documents The registered agent is required to be the official Secretary of State person-in-charge and should be at the designated physical address within specified business times. It is essential to ensure that your registered agent is available anytime. The absence of this document can damage the relationship between your business and the government, and even worse the state could let the filing of a suit against you to be filed even when you're not in the office.

After that, you need to be able to obtain an EIN number. It is also called your company's employer identification number. EIN numbers, similar to Social Security numbers could be used to differentiate and identify companies. The nine-digit code is needed for opening a bank account. It must be included on your business's tax return.

The need to obtain the required licenses and permits

Get all permits required and permits. When you've established your company and obtained business permits and permits. The regulations vary for each sector, region and the state.

Declare Your Company. Certain states, including Arizona as well as New York, require you to announce the LLC establishment in your local paper.

The name implies the business is a solo company. It's the simplest type of business since it doesn't require the registration of any other type, except for licences or permits within your field.

Pros

It's easy to start as there's no sign-up necessary.

Making decisions are quick since there's no requirement for consulting. It is not possible to double tax as the business and owner are considered to be one entity. Therefore, the income of business can be reported on a personal tax return.

Only the revenue generated by the company is taxed.

If the company earns a revenue, the proprietor gets to keep the entire amount since the owner is the sole owner.

Cons

In the event that the firm isn't able to meet its obligations and liability, the personal assets, like the car or your house may be used as a way to reduce them.

The taxes on Social Security and Medicare are twice what you pay when you are an employee.

If the business suffers financial losses, the business's owner is the sole responsible. There isn't any separation between you and your business the business, getting a loan for your business from a bank is a challenge.

Because of the ease that they are able to be set up Due to the ease of establishing them, most startups can be sole-proprietorships. Since there's no distinction between the proprietor as well as the company the liability is unlimitable that can prove extremely hazardous. This is why many of these firms transform into LLCs or corporate entities.

Making an operating contract

Operating agreements are an agreement between members of the LLC which governs the LLC and its terms, rules as well as the dos and don'ts and also the members' obligations and rights.

There are not all states that in the United States require LLCs to possess a written Operating Contract. As of now, the following states need written Operating Agreements to LLCs active or registered in their respective states:

New Mexico, Arkansas, and Washington, DC. are required to have a written Operating Agreement, unless otherwise stipulated by the Articles of Organization. Connecticut, Colorado, Kentucky as well as Georgia are required to have a written Operating Agreement for multi-member LLCs (LLCs that have at least two members). This requirement is not applicable to SMLLCs.

In addition to the states mentioned above the majority of other US state laws aren't addressing the matter of operating agreements in writing for LLCs, or only require them under certain circumstances.

Although your state may not require LLCs to sign an Operating Agreement however, it is recommended that all LLCs have and have a customized Operating Agreement. If your LLC doesn't have an Operating Agreement the default state LLC law will govern. It could or might not serve your interests.

LLCs do not have to submit their Operating Agreement at any government agency. Instead, they are required to maintain an Operating Agreement and adhere to the Operating Agreement for the management of the LLC and save the Operating Agreement within the business documents of the LLC.

It is also required by state law or the SMLLC has also been required under the law of the state or is strongly encouraged to draft and adopt the Operating Agreement as a reference governance document. However, the SMLLC is comprised of only one person which is unlikely to disagree with one another or face issues regarding the distribution of profits from the SMLLC. Therefore, the significance of an Operating Agreement in an SMLLC (a single-person business) can be called to be in doubt. But, the Operating Agreement is highly recommended in the SMLLC for its plan and administration instrument.

In the majority of states in many states, the MMLLC is legally required or is strongly urged by professionals to create and implement operating Agreement to serve as a reference document that is primarily used to resolve disagreements between members concerning the MMLLC's management and policies as well as (ii) be clear about the MMLLC's capital contribution as well as distribution guidelines and formulas to members. members.

The document (the Operating Agreement) has been proven useful and efficient with MMLLC members (as as opposed members who are single-members members of SMLLC).

Since there is a chance that Federal Motor Carrier Safety Administration (FMCSA) may ask you questions regarding your business operations First, you need to make sure that your business is legal before making an application for an USDOT Number.

For starters, visit your state's Secretary of States' website, and then search their database to determine if the firm's name is in the database. Next, you must decide on a structure for your business.

Most likely, you'll create a sole proprietorship, or Limited Liability Corporation if you're setting up a company on the basis of your own. However, there are various other structures for business that you can think about. For more information on how to start your own business is available on the Small Business Association.

Sole proprietorships are single-person company that does not have employees or is independent of the proprietor.

Since you are a sole proprietor you are able to decide on all business matters on solely, without the help of a partner or Board of Directors. It is a disadvantage that you're the sole owner of all legal and financial aspects of the company. In the event that you are sued by your business or you are facing debt-related issues the personal assets of your family could be in danger.

An LLC can provide the same tax benefits like a sole proprietorship but with no risk of personal responsibility. In an LLC, the business's responsibility is held while your personal assets are secure. Single-member LLCs, partnership or multi-member LLC can be considered as viable alternatives.

Obtain Employer Identification Number (EIN)

It is also known as the Employer Identification Number (EIN) is sometimes referred to The Federal Tax Identification Number (FTIN). It's a nine-digit code which is employed to determine the identity of a company in tax-related reasons. The possession of an EIN lets you open corporate accounts as well as obtain licenses. EINs are required to open business accounts and obtain licences. EIN is available through the internet. The IRS will be asking you some simple questions that you'll have to answer. It is the most straightforward and fastest way to obtain EIN. EIN.

In order to apply to apply for an EIN You must provide these details: name as well as the Taxpayer Identification number of the business's owner principal officer, general partner. The person in charge of the application must be the person responsible for managing and managing the company's assets. It is not possible to accomplish this by using an entity for business.

Register for State Tax

Every business that operates within a state is tax obligations. If there are employees in the business who are state employees, they must pay taxes on sales, income as well as employment tax.

First, you must make an application for tax registration by registering with the state's revenue department. Certain states, like Washington, South Dakota, and Florida don't have any income tax. Make sure to determine the state in which you reside that requires the payment of income tax.

An organization that offers products or services required to pay sales tax has to be eligible for a tax sales license in the state where it operates. Sales tax can also be called an tax on trust funds. The permit permits the collection, reporting and even pay sales tax in the state. Many states provide an online registration process. Alaska, Delaware, and Montana are among those states that don't levy sales tax.

If you are a taxpayer with a presence in a state, and employ employees, you're obliged by law to be registered with the employment bureau of your state. This allows the state to collect taxes on income for the state from the employees. Also, you have to pay tax on unemployment for the state and also to pay into the worker's compensation fund.

Important: If you do your business in multiple states it is necessary to register with each state separately for taxes. The state where you initially register your company is considered to be a domestic business company. The other states are where you have to register as a foreign company.

Income Tax

Each business has to pay income tax on profits. Your business's nature is the determining factor in how you pay the tax. Sole proprietorship is for instance, and requires the addition of the net earnings from Schedule C along with your revenue from different sources to figure the tax amount you will pay. LLC owners on the however are able to choose paying taxes either as a sole proprietor, or as a corporate. This means that those who own LLCs and pay taxes as a sole proprietor is likely to have a different amount of tax that a business with similar income.

For business owners The law permits you to deduct certain costs prior to declaring your tax-deductible earnings. There are a variety of company expenses that you can deduct.

It is crucial to make sure that you are able to deduct only costs incurred to support business. The most important thing is to be able to prove each deduction that you take. Some of the costs you can be able to deduct are:

• Meals and snacks for business. Business insurance.

Travel and expenses related to work. Promotions and advertisements.

Cleaning and accounting are two examples of services that professionals provide.

Another kind of deduction for business. It's known as qualified deduction for business profits (QBI). The law came into force during the tax year 2018 and is in force through 2025. The tax deduction is up to 20% of your qualified profits from your business with QBI (Murray 2020). This deduction, however, is only available to owners of businesses who have their taxes paid through their personal tax returns.

Self-Employment Taxes

Taxes on self-employment contribute to funding Social Security as well as Medicare. What you are required to pay for taxes is calculated by the net revenue of the company, exactly like the income tax. It means that you will pay no tax on self-employment if the business does not earn any profits. The tax does not stop at that point. If you fail to make self-employment tax payments and you do not receive Social Security or Medicare benefits during the current year. If you wish to grow your Social

Security and Medicare credits every year, it is essential to continue making profit.

The sole proprietors, the members of a partnership and LLC owners must pay self-employment tax.

Sales Tax

Sales tax is imposed on certain products and services that are sold by business. The government imposes a percentage tax for the sale of specific items as well as services. It is good to know that the tax is not the responsibility of the business owner. The consumers have to pay.

The job of a firm is to collect this tax, record it and then pay it back to the authorities. In order to avoid mistakenly interpreting the tax as revenue or profits, you need an effective system to record and collect the tax.

Gross Receipts Tax

As we've discussed previously, the majority of states impose on businesses the obligation to pay state income taxes. Some states, like Nevada as well as Texas are able to impose a gross revenue (revenue) tax. This is either a supplement or replacement for the income tax imposed by the state.

Certain types of companies are eligible for gross income tax. Therefore, it is important to inquire in with your state the eligibility of your business for the tax. The sole proprietor is usually not eligible to pay the tax on gross receipts even though they pay taxes on their incomes to the state.

issuing membership certificates as a reward to invest the shareholders of a company receive shares. The ownership of an LLC, however will be in the form membership interest, not stock. In this way, certain LLCs will issue certificates of membership to their members to prove ownership of the business.

If you decide to distribute membership interest certificates the operating agreement you sign will clearly outline the goal and procedure for distributing the certificates. It is

possible to give membership certificates in accordance with the percentage of ownership each member has and you could also design a specific number of membership units to give these to members in accordance with the membership interest of each member.

A company isn't legally required to issue certificates of membership interest. If you choose to issue membership interest certificates it's important to note the price of a membership interest is to be specified in the operating agreement. Every participant in your LLC is required to contribute capital to the company in exchange for an agreed amount of membership units, or a proportional ownership stake in the firm.

The LLC can create an unlimited number of membership units. The ledger of membership transfers keeps the track of every member's membership interests. Members don't need to have certificates in order to demonstrate ownership of the corporation since members' interests stem from the contract between members as well as the LLC. The certificates of interest for membership are required to be listed in the application.

The importance of each member certificate

The process of granting certificates

Each certificate is a fraction of interest in membership.

While an LLC isn't mandated by law to issue interest certificates for members It is advisable to make this decision in certain situations. This is particularly true when you plan to raise capital later on by selling membership certificates to investors.

An LLC with a smaller number of owners and does not plan to draw investors might not be required issues certificate of membership interests. Large LLC that is seeking investors, however must issue membership certificates as the types of membership interest the investor is able to acquire is restricted. It is necessary to issue members' interest in order in order to make the restrictions legal applicable.

Transfer restrictions

There are provisions to reverse vest

Buy-sell clauses

Chapter 2: Managing Your Llc

In order to manage the affairs of an LLC to manage an LLC, first create the LLC first, and then set up the payment allocation process as well as an operating agreement and, if needed insure your personal assets. LLCs can provide small personal protections that corporations offer without the burdensome requirements for a corporate structure. In addition, LLCs are more costly to set up. This is a great choice for those that do not plan to invest a substantial amount of funds.

Allocation System

LLCs have a unique profit distribution, that is the share that members receive of earnings based on the level of ownership. This is also referred to as guaranteed payment. It also permits members to make checks payable to themselves when they require cash, however only when the LLC is cash-flow positive. Additionally, members can record profits in their tax return as well as deduct losses.

Additionally, since the controlling member is classified as an non-active proprietor, their part of any profit that is bottom-line not considered earned income. This gives the member tax-free advantages. Every member in a guaranteed payment scheme earns income which allows them to make use of fringe benefits with tax advantages.

Creating an LLC

The articles of association are the basis of the basis of your LLC and need to be registered with the state's LLC corporation division. The corporation division is typically affiliated with the Secretary of State's Office. The fees vary, however they typically range from $100 to $1000.

States generally provide the form for one page on which you can fill in essential information regarding the LLC. Information should contain the following:

Name, Address, and Contact Information

Registered Representative

Certain states may need you to record the names and addresses of all LLC members name as well as addresses.

Operating Agreement

A operating agreement outlines the basic structure of your business's management. This isn't a legal document that has to be filed with the authorities, however you must create an operating agreement to ensure the organization as well as to ensure that everyone members know the roles they play and their responsibilities. Additionally, the compensation program must be included within the operating agreement, so everyone is aware of the ways in which they are paid, and what percentage of the company.

EIN

The IRS employs EINs for identifying and taxing the business. The need for an EIN number from the federal government is vital for a variety of motives, among them:

Employee Recruitment

If you have multiple members You can get the free EIN on the IRS site. The EIN is also needed when opening a bank account in a company.

Dividing Business and Personal Assets

While some states do not allow the practice, many people create sole-member LLCs to gain a brand new EIN as well as a brand new credit line. However, in any event, you must avoid the blending of personal and business credit lines. Therefore, if the borrower is granted the collateral or funds through his personal credit score, they should consult your account for the proper documentation of the transactions.

Always keep an unbreakable barrier between your both business and personal matters regardless of the method by which credit is derived. Even with LLC individual liability protections failing to follow this advice can put the LLC to liability under the law. When members have a mix of personal and professional actions, certain creditor and courts have been able to work over LLC law regarding liability.

Insurance

If LLC laws don't protect the assets of your company, you may purchase a sound insurance policy that will. In the case, for instance, you are massage therapist and hurt clients, the insurance coverage will cover your assets in case that you are sued. In addition, insurance is an asset that is worth having when a court fails to respect the protections you have for liability. Insurance also helps protect business and business assets from judgments as well as lawsuits.

In this respect, it is vital to know that commercial insurance cannot safeguard personal or business property that is the result of unpaid corporate debts, regardless whether these assets are personal secured.

Paperwork

Regular filings and annual documents are necessary for the running in an LLC. In the case of an instance the LLC located in Michigan has to renew each year and in the event that you do not submit your paperwork on time, the LLC might be terminated. Therefore it is your responsibility to ensure your LLC's articles of organization remain in good order and that any amendments made to the LLC have been incorporated in the form of a letter to the IRS as well as your state. In the event of signing any corporate documents make sure you use your full business name, with the proper suffix (LLC, L.L.C, etc.) and add your name as a shareholder of the LLC as well as your name as the company's official title.

Are you interested in learning more about the management of an LLC? For more details, you can submit your request for legal advice to UpCounsel. UpCounsel marketplace. Our attorneys from UpCounsel can guide you through the procedure of management and will help you find the most effective ways to safeguard your assets, both personal and corporate. They will also help you with planning your emergency plans like lawsuits and guide through difficult situations in order to let you focus on the business aspects.

Knowing the responsibilities and roles of LLC members

If you are an LLC member, the responsibilities and roles you have as an LLC member depend on your operating agreement as well as law in the state that govern the place where your LLC is registered. LLC members are able to participate in managing the company, or may delegate managerial duties to managers or managing team.

LLC members are those who invest funds or other assets in the company to assist it in its efforts to grow.LLC members enjoy limited liability protection. This means they don't have to personally be accountable for any debts or obligations above the amount of their investment.LLC members are involved in decisions that impact the company, for example approving contracts, making decisions on the distribution of earnings and losses, as well as taking votes on any modifications to the operating agreement.

LLC members have the responsibility of the payment of taxes on their portion of the profits made by the LLC and also filing the necessary documents and keeping accurate accounting records.LLC members have a duty to behave in the best interest of the LLC as well as its members and to stay clear of conflicts of interest and use the appropriate care when acting in the name members of the LLC.

It's crucial to understand that the role and responsibility of LLC members are a bit different in accordance with the type of enterprise and the mission that are set by the LLC. Furthermore, LLC members can choose to assign some aspects of their duties to members of the management team or to others members and this can affect the extent to which they are involved with the daily operations of their business.

Meetings and keeping minutes

The holding of meetings and the recording of the minutes are essential aspects of running the operations of an LLC.

Meet as needed

In accordance with the terms of your operating agreement as well as state law, LLCs could be required to host specific types of meetings like annual or other special gatherings. Be sure to adhere to these rules to remain within the law.

It is important to inform everyone members of meetings scheduled prior to the meeting, including the date, time, and the location along with an agenda for the event.

Document meeting minutes

Minutes must be recorded at each meeting. They should contain a synopsis of the meeting, any decision taken, as well as any action to be performed. Minutes must be recorded in the LLC's records.Keep precise records: Keeping complete records of meetings and the decisions taken is essential in both financial and legal reasons. This can assist in the resolution of disputes as well as ensuring that there is transparency in the LLC.

If you have any questions or concerns raised at the time of the meeting, make sure to resolve them quickly and record any actions or decisions made to resolve them.

Record keeping and maintaining the books of account

Document archive is a continuous procedure. The process of archiving documents requires funds for its setup and maintenance. There will be some costs related to this within your budget but the advantages mentioned above will be more than compensating.

1. Initial evaluation

Review the procedure you are currently using for document management and process. Do you have a formal or informal, or a mixture of both? It will also include the making and processing of each record, as well as receipt as well as the storage and deletion of the record.

It is also necessary to take inventory of your existing records for the purpose of calculating the total amount. Each document, which includes documents related to finances and personnel, as well as shipping as well as insurance, Receiving, and other tasks should be categorize according to the function they serve.

2. Establish your expectations and responsibilities.

Set your goals for document storage crystal clear. Do you want to reduce daily operating costs? Do you meet the record-keeping and data security laws?

Verify that the routine office processes are completed with greater efficiency. Utilize online document storage services for making it easy to search for old documents. Enhancing your business's metrics

You're sure to want all of these but, to ensure that your archive efforts stay up to date, you have to make them a priority.

It is also important to have the roles for each organization established. Beyond initial supervision Who will be accountable for the ongoing archive process? What level of authorization do you intend to use to limit access to archived information? How can you convince your employees to adhere?

3. Establish the retention plan.

If you're conscious of the objectives you want to achieve in archiving, and you have decided on the person the person who will carry out and supervise the archiving plan, you can create an action plan to preserve the company's documents.

Apart from records like annual financial reports or deeds that must be maintained for a long time, the majority of documents last not more than 10 years.

There's no standard in the industry to retain commercial documents. Learn about the guidelines that need to be observed at the federal, local as well as state and sectoral level. It is a good idea to follow the practice of preserving the IRS and tax-related documents for seven years.

Then, you must get rid of the documents you don't want to be saved or cannot be stored.

The duplicate copies of vendor catalogues, duplicate copies and junk mail such as, for instance, shouldn't be stored indefinitely.

For a lower risk of liability, choose for liability reduction, choose a National Association of Info Destruction (NAID) service for security of transportation, destruction and disposal.

Step 4. Convert your paper-based files into digital format.

If you digitize all the hard-copy information you have it will help you cut expenses and storage space, and also streamline the organization as well as improving access. Documents must be maintained in hardcopy format, however, they must also be made digital for security reasons.

In the beginning, at least for configuration in the first stage of setting up the document repository the use of an office worker who is not paid is less effective rather than utilizing a specialist third-party vendor.

In order to make sure that documents are available to all Save them in open file formats like PDF or ODT for documents. SVG and PNG for images as well as ODS for spreadsheets.

If you have saved your files using a proprietary format, but it isn't in use or you do not possess the license to access it, you might have difficulty opening files in the near future.

Make use of metadata or other details regarding the content of the digital file each file.

Since metadata lets you include information such as the document's title, author, a brief description, keywords and many more, it can aid in organizing your documents as well as facilitate access in the future. It is usually possible to retrieve metadata when you right-click a document then selecting "Properties" or "Get details" according to your operating system.

Step 5: Choose a storage vendor.

The safest method to store records is to make use of the services of a third party provider's off-site backups or digital data storage. These storage facilities are protected against natural as well as man-made events like burglary, unauthorised access flooding, earthquakes, and floods. To store your electronic files there are three main choices: cloud, disc and soldotape. Each of them has pros and cons regarding longevity, integrity, security as well as the ease of access for record management software. Think about combining two methods to make sure that data is redundant.

Step 6: Compare the internal and external storage.

Retention and archiving of documents is a continual process that is ongoing. Re-evaluate your practices annually in your general policy in order to evaluate the effectiveness of your processes and to make any changes that are needed.

Each employee is required to contribute to the effective preservation and archive of records. Apart from other education, make use of communication methods including an overview of policies at the time of beginning of the year and refresher sessions each year.

Also, ensure the security and accessibility of the archived data regularly. What you don't want to learn is that you have an issue regarding your archive storage to be able to access the data in a tax audit, the court of law, or following an event of natural catastrophe.

Tax filing and annual reports

It's important to know the fact that the annual report of an LLC annual report isn't identical to the extensive annual financial reports that large corporations issue to shareholders, analysts as well as regulators every year.

The LLC annual report in contrast gives the basic details about your company, including your address and the names of the registered agent, directors and supervisors. It's a comprehensive report about the business's operations during the year prior. The annual report is designed to educate shareholders and other individuals who may be interested in the activities of the company as well as financial performance.

States have a requirement for annual filings as they feel it's essential for this data to be readily available to the public since the details of an organization can change during the course of a year. In addition, many states gather financial data about the LLC to determine the amount of franchise tax they may have to pay.

Penalties for failing to file the LLC annual statement?

If you file late, or not even filing at all can result in consequences. The penalty for late filing is generally penalized in the majority of states. In addition, your company may not remain in good standing with the state until submission is made. It could affect your business' capability to secure finance, end contracts or even expand its business.

If you are waiting too long, the home state could dissolve your business, or a state outside of your home (a state where you conduct commercial operations that aren't in the state you are based in) could revoke your rights to conduct business in that state.

Limited liability protection for your LLC will no longer be available after the LLC is dissolved. The loss of good standing could be detrimental to your organization's capacity to take an action in a state court like suing another person in violation of the contract.

What is the information that must be contained in the annual report? While the requirements for information vary from state to state the annual report usually contains the following details:

Your official name for the company you work for

For an overseas company, it is the fake name that it was registered under in the first instance, should be used.

If it is applicable If applicable, the main office of the state address.

The office's location is the same wherever it's in the area, this address is its address.

Name of the registered agent

The location of the registered office

The addresses and names of LLC's management as well as members

Knowing the franchise tax

Franchise taxes, in spite of their title, aren't charged to franchises. States instead impose franchise taxes on companies to allow them to be established or registered to carry out business in the state. Think of it as the cost imposed by the state for giving your LLC the legal authority needed to be a part of that state. You can also enjoy the benefits associated with having an LLC.

The method of calculating franchise tax is different based on the state where the LLC was formed as well as the type of company which you run. The tax is usually calculated using income from business as well as business assets. the amount of shares outstanding of corporate stock as well as the par value of each share. This can also be determined by combining the above factors.

Conforming to federal and state rules and laws

The liability of an individual is strictly limited. The obligations, debts or liabilities paid for or otherwise related to the Trust and the series or class are not personal liability for Shareholders in the event of the conduct of their own. Except as expressly stated in the Agreement and the Trust's Bylaws, no one of the trustees or the Trust and its personnel, officers or representatives of the Trust are authorized to make any shareholder personally liable or demand any amount from any Shareholder, other than what the

Shareholder can in any moment individually agree to. Imagine a privately-owned for-profit corporation founded in Delaware includes shareholders.

In this case, shareholders will be at risk of personal liability caps for as long as the amount exceeds the cap on liability set in this section. One of the most significant benefits is the formation of a real estate Limited Liability Company (LLC).

Establishing your real estate company for a home buyer or other an investment company in real estate offers a number of advantages. Four advantages worth considering:

Chapter 3: Funding Your Llc

The proper funding of your business is an important aspect of setting up a successful Limited Liability Company (LLC). A lot of new companies fail due to the fact that they don't have the money to cover the beginning phase. A thorough, efficient business plan will help find funds by proving to future lenders and investors your capacity to make loans repayable or attain profit over the course of time. There are a variety of options available for financing your LLC but here are the top options to think about.

Evaluate Your Own Assets.

Most entrepreneurs who are considering starting a business look at their own personal wealth for funding their venture whether that's through liquidation or making them collateral for loan. There are times when you might be able make use of your own savings in cash and then sell real or personal property for example, your home to help fund the new LLC. If you are able to get equity from your house, you may look into obtaining an equity loan for your home for your business in order to finance it. If you're in a position to not make mortgage payment, you'll have to forfeit not just your brand new company, but also your home. If you own retirement accounts and retirement accounts, you might have the option of borrowing through them over a short amount of time to help finance the start-up. There could be huge withdrawal charges as well as tax consequences for taking money and not paying it in the timeframes required.

Contact Your Personal Network for Informal Loans.

Most entrepreneurs have discussed the idea of starting the business of their own with the family or acquaintances. The closest relationships you have with your family and friends are those within your social and family circles. The people who know you well will be more inclined to place their faith in you, and the money they invest in your business. The informal funding may be easy to get, however it can cause long-term issues with your family or social relationships should it not be paid back. If you're willing to take the possibility of risk then it might be worth to ask for financial aid through your own circle.

Invite New Members to Your LLC Team

Inviting new members might be a option to help fund your startup. While you might want to do it on your own take into consideration the advantages that include others LLC members as well as owners to your business for financing purposes. Your fellow members are able to join together your resources in order for your business. Also, your LLC can broaden its networking network with business connections as well as potential investors, by joining your fellow members. In addition to generating more money to fund your LLC New members can also bring benefits of taking advantage of the experience of other members.

Consider credit cards for short-term financing Many individuals like the original Google founders Google could try to launch their business using private credit cards. Numerous credit card companies offer credit cards for businesses with minimal or no annual charges with competitive interest rates as well as travel rewards, and cash-back on purchases made by businesses. Credit cards are able to provide instant credit with no need for loans as well as business-related plans. Since interest rates on credit cards can be very expensive, entrepreneurs who have just started their business could want to look into credit cards as a short-term solution to meet

LLC requirements that must be paid off as fast as it is feasible. Beware of accumulating huge amounts of debt from credit cards which can make the finance process costly over the long term.

Apply for Conventional Loans From Institutional Lenders.

It is possible to go down the conventional way and request loans through banks and credit unions. A business plan that is formalized is required as a part of the loan procedure. A lot of traditional lenders are skeptical of entrepreneurs who aren't experienced Don't be shocked when you receive a number of rejections. The borrowing against collateral you already have could boost your chances of getting finance, but it'll almost certainly be a tough route. If you opt to borrow the assets you have as collateral to get an institution-based loan, bear your eyes on the fact that if you don't pay back these loans to business then you'll forfeit your primary collateral.

Check Out Government-Sponsored Grant and Loan Programs.

State, federal, and local government agencies may provide specific loan or grant programs to assist you in financing your business with traditional intermediaries or non-profit lenders. The government may sponsor programs that target

1.) particular sectors, like alternative energy sources,

2.) certain business owners, like military veterans

3.) certain geographic regions that are economically depressed communities

4.) certain dollars, for example microloans that start with $100. There are four specific dollar amounts, such as microloans starting at $100. Small Business Administration (SBA) has an online search tool to locate programs for grants and loans which could be suitable for your business idea.

Get connected with Peer-toPeer Lending Websites.

Peer-to-peer (P2P) also known as social lending sites have popped up on the Internet over the last few time. These P2P websites allow entrepreneurs who are creditworthy to request financing from institutional or private investors. On these sites they allow you to apply for loans online. investors who have accounts with them will decide whether to finance your business through loan that are based on interest. The peer-to-peer (P2P) sites offer online alternatives to traditional lenders and are anticipated to increase as fast, secure source of business financing. Lending Club and Prosper are two of the most well-known P2P websites.

Learning about the different funding sources

Savings for personal expenses

LLC owners are able to utilize their own savings to finance their venture. Owners of family and friends LLC may seek financial assistance from acquaintances and family members who would like to put money into the company.

Angel investors

The angel investors include wealthy people who invest in startup companies or small-sized businesses. They usually invest in the beginning stages of business and also provide the seed capital. Venture capital companies invest in businesses with significant potential for growth. They generally invest in companies who have achieved a certain amount of progress and want to grow.

Small Business Administration (SBA) credit

The SBA gives business loans for small enterprises such as LLCs, in order for them to start or develop their businesses. Crowdfunding platforms permit LLC owners to get money from a wide range of individuals who are keen to help their idea for business. LLC owners may make an application for conventional banks to fund their business activities.

Capital raising through equity or credit financing

Members of a partnership are responsible for their own personal liability for obligations incurred by the company and also for the conduct of other members. The Limited Liability Company, on its own, is able to divide the assets and liabilities of its members in a way that each of the members aren't personally responsible to them. The format of the company shields its owners from personal responsibility.

There are however limitations to the separation between the business and personal liability of an LLC. This is the case instances where:

at least one business insurance participant.

The line between corporations and people is a wave. The owner engages in a fraudulent or unlawful act.

One member at least is bully-like in concerns related to business. All members agree that they will be personally accountable for financial obligations.

Differ as One-Person LLCs

Taxes are paid as sole owners. Schedule C: Schedule C must be filed alongside an individual tax return.

A limited liability business (LLC) which has at least one members could choose to tax as a S or a corporation in lieu of a.

An LLC Tax Status

Every legal way of conducting business comes with a tax classification that is associated with the method, and specific rules and regulations applicable to the various types of companies. The consequences of legal liability is not the main focus of this post however, it is important to mention them in order to explain why some people opt to create the Limited Liability Company and why this may not be the most appropriate choice.

The most basic forms that are available to small-sized businesses are outlined in this article.

A corporation that is incorporated with only one owner with no legal distinction between the two entities, i.e., unlimited legal obligation. Non-incorporated business owners are required to file Schedule C returns, which can be found in individual tax return.

1. Partnership: A different unincorporated partnership that has the same unlimited legal obligation for sole proprietorship, the partnership is comprised of several owners (the proprietor does not need to be a person and I'll leave the rules simple) and file the tax return using form 1065. Every partner is issued a K1 describing the amount of revenue as well as expenses and details that the partnership declares in their personal tax return.

2. C-Corp A corporate entity that is not controlled by shareholders. The owners have a limited liability under the law this means

that they're not in danger from conducting business outside their own companies. However, it is important to note that there are always some exceptions to this policy however I don't deal with legal liability issues.

3. S-Corp is the same thing as C-corp, however with no tax advantages of a corporation. It does not have corporate tax. A shareholder gets the form K1 from the company and then reports his personal tax return, the amount of his taxes as well as deductions and other documents.

We're at LLC. It is simply an unincorporated business. The owners/owners have the same liability limitations like their shareholders. This is fantastic in the context of taxes. There is no doubt there's no tax class. The IRS offers an "default" classification to LLCs.

I'll clarify number of tax-related issues. When it comes to taxation the single-member LLC is sole owner. It has two main disadvantages. First the sole proprietors are more likely than companies to be scrutinized through the IRS.

The second reason is that profits are subject to taxation to Social Security Administration. Social Security Administration.

The partnership is the most common type of business that will submit the return with Form 1065. Also, even if partners haven't earned income, the earnings of all parties are dependent on social security tax. Keep in mind the fact that social security tax is calculated of "active" income and does not apply to activities like property ownership. Additionally, the LLC that has multiple members isn't part of the partnership.

They're great in certain scenarios, for instance the purchase of property. It is my opinion that you'd prefer to join the ranks because it sounds interesting. It's the latest style. The tax consequences until it's to late. In the majority of cases the S-corp is what you need, that's the most efficient option for the small-scale business.

IRS Form 8832 may be employed to apply for relief. The form has to be submitted within 75 days from the date of creation In the event of a delay, failure to comply could lead to late election relief.

1. Microbusiness success centres: The most effective microbusiness solution in the world. Small-scale business owners are able to become leaders of their own companies through adopting our philosophy and taking advantage of our products and services. Companies have turned into valuable, sellable assets, which will help the owners with investment.

2. Pro-Biz aid Incorporated assists those in their quest for financial and personal success with information, clear direction, tools and other resources that help people realize their potential to the fullest extent.

3. Pro Bookkeepers Inc.: Utilizing the latest technology along with our years of expertise in administration of the office, scheduling and customer support We will work with you in providing all the tools you need for running

your business instead of managing your company.

4. Pro Micro Business Marketing Our specialist team in marketing specializes on micro-business-specific marketing. Advertising and marketing can be costly and time-consuming, but also don't meet the demands of micro-business owners.

The process of creating a business strategy and financial projections

If you're planning to operate your company as a sole proprietorship, there's no need to develop a business plan as you would if planning to fund the form of a Limited Liability Company, but I'd recommend you have one. What differentiates one sole proprietorship as opposed to an LLC is the fact that an LLC Limited Liability Company is considered as an established company by the federal government. It can be costly to start a business. It has a number of advantages. The most significant of which is the tax benefits as well as the legal security it affords. I highly recommend you create an LLC instead of managing your business solely as a owner.

A business plan is an outline that you use to write down the goals of your company, the ways you'll achieve these targets, and the length of time it's going to take. The business plan will also outline the nature of your business, its financial projections, as well as the actions you plan to follow to reach those objectives.

It is essential to create the business plan as it defines your business's goals as well as the methods you'll employ in order to accomplish these goals. The plan is a blueprint to achieve success. You could sit back and go about your business until you're running your business to the ground, if you don't have a clear idea of your objectives and the best way to achieve them. It is more likely that you will achieve success if you've got an action plan that is clear.

It must at most include a recent budget.

An estimate of sales for the next 3 years. A strategy for sales and production. Research on the market.

The budgeted costs for the coming three years that are linked to the budget you have in place.

Profit and loss accounts. Analyzing break-even points

A description for the group (strengths and ways to deal the weaknesses and manage these).

SWOT (strengths strengths, weaknesses, risks, and opportunities pertaining to your company) (strengths and weaknesses potential threats, and strengths related to your business).

The summary of the product or service. The statement of mission.

Vision statement.

If you're developing your business plan to attract investors, you'll require an income forecast. This isn't required but it is a must if your business plan is solely for you.

While creating your business plan take into consideration how much you'll need to spend in order to meet certain business milestones and where you're at in your journey, and the best way to move from the current position towards where you would like to get there. It is also important to find the most effective way to get your message out to the market. There are a variety of marketing methods that you can choose from; however, you should decide which one is the most efficient for your market. Additionally, it is advantageous to establish connections with small-sized business owners that you are able to contract out to complete work.

Every company is distinctive. Strategies for selling goods and services can differ depending upon the business type. The strategies will vary according to the item or service. It is necessary to have a strategy to each and your business plan can assist you in achieving your goal.

There may be multiple areas that fall within the umbrella of your company's brand. The norm is that each department will require an individual marketing plan. Your brand, for instance, might include both a house remodeling division as well as an investment department. Strategies for marketing you use to draw remodeling projects are different in comparison to the ones you use to grow your portfolio of investment assets.

Chapter 4: Expanding Your Llc

If your business is quickly growing, you might want to think about expanding outside the limits of your own state. This article will help you be aware of about this process.

A small-sized business may expand into a new location without the need to create an entirely new structure or company.

Certain states are more welcoming to business than others, however there are rules for businesses everywhere that they have to follow.

Plan in advance to make sure you have an easy relocation or expansion.

This post is aimed at entrepreneurs who have thought of expanding their business to a new state.

It's time to expand your growing company into a different state. First, you need to make sure that you are in compliance with applicable laws and put the business up for success. Here are all the details when expanding to a new state, to help you understand the procedure and make sure that you are on the right track.

Independent contractors or employees who hire hiring personnel.

An LLC has the option of hiring LLC employees as well as using independent contractors. Both can provide you with skills as well as help expand your company, however the tax treatment is different for each. Employing independent contractors is the ideal choice if you do not need to worry about tax payments (or even getting benefits) on behalf of the employee.

Difference Between Employees and Independent Contractors?

Find out the main differences between employees and contractors in order to find the best people for your company.

A worker is employed by a business and earns salary as well as benefits in return for adhering to company's guidelines and staying loyal.

Contractors are self-employed one who can work independently and with flexibility, but doesn't receive advantages like health insurance, or the opportunity to take paid vacation.

Fines, back taxes penalties, back taxes, and litigation can arise because of misclassifying an employee.

This post is aimed at those who run businesses and want to learn how to categorize their staff.

A contract worker, rather as a full-time employee could reduce your costs for the company; for one thing, you will not need to provide medical insurance, 401(k) matches, holiday hours, or any other benefits. The decision to do this, however there are limitations and risk. When deciding on which kind of worker you will need to fulfill a particular job It is essential to be aware of the differentiators between workers and contractors in addition to the implications in the event of misclassifying workers.

In the case of the hiring of independent contractors, or employees, there's a number of factors to be considered.

If you choose to hire someone for an all-time (permanent) job and the federal government considers the person an employee of the business. But, if you wish to employ an employee on a temporary or projectbyproject basis, they will be considered to be an independent contractor.

The hiring of independent contractors (also referred to as freelancers) instead of employees offers tax benefits. If you employ independent contractors, your LLC does not have to be responsible for paying taxes for the contractor (regardless whether they're an individual or the company employed).

Process for Hiring Independent Contractors?

In the event that you decide to hire an independent contractor in order to alleviate the pressure on you There are some types you must fill out to become familiar with. These forms should be completed prior to any work begins to be done in order to make sure that those employed as independent contractors are not considered employees.

1. Form W-9

The independent contractor should be given the W-9 form to complete. This form gives you the Taxpayer Identification Number (TIN) and name as well as their address. It could refer to the individuals Social Security number (SSN) or an Employer Identification Number (EIN) when they run a business.

2. 1099-MISC Form

If you are planning to pay your contractor over $600 within the course of a calendar year, it is required to file a 1099MISC (Miscellaneous income) report with the IRS. Although the contractor is accountable for paying their own taxes however, you need to supply the contractor with a single duplicate of the form, and the IRS with a duplicate (both are due by the end of January for a specific year).

3. Form 1096

This is a form that you use for your business, and is also known as the Annual Summary, Transmittal and Report of US Information Tax Returns. It is required to fill out this form and mail it back in Social Security Administration by the end of February. Social Security

Administration by the deadline of February 31st, with copies of the 1099s from contractors who have that earned over $600 for the entire year.

The Pros of Hiring Independent Contractors

Could save you as well as the business you run

Lowers the risk of getting sued

It also gives you a degree of flexibility.

Lets you outsource your projects without tax liability

The Cons of Hiring Independent Contractors

The contractor has no influence over them.

If there isn't any the time to work with them then they could find employment elsewhere.

Terminating a contractor should be handled with care and in accordance to the termination clause of the contract.

If employees are injured in the course of their work the business could be held accountable for any injuries

Certain contractors have all rights related to the work they have completed

The IRS is able to audit your business in order to make sure contractors are utilized as such instead of being employed as employees

Contracts and agreements are entered into.

A partnership is a contract with two or more persons to manage and run an enterprise while sharing the profits. It is possible to register your brokerage company under various agreement for partnership. Profits and liabilities are split equally between the partners of partnership agreements, as well as under any other share agreement signed in by the partners. This is especially true for partnership agreements where some of the partners only have a limited liabilities. There are three kinds of partnerships that you could form:

General collaboration. Limited liability business. Partnership that has a limited liability.

The profits and the liabilities are divided equally within the general partnership. Every partner personally is responsible to the partnership's obligations and debts. obligations. The profits and losses are divided equally, or according to the provisions of the agreement between partners.

Professionals are often part of limited partnership with a limited liability. Lawyers, doctors as well as architects and accountants are some of them. Because of that they are not liable when one of the partners suffers legal damage because of malpractice, or for any other cause, the assets of other partners are in no way affected.

Limited partnerships are hybrids between limited and general liability partnerships. There must be at least one general partner for the partnership. The general partner assumes personal responsibility for company's debts.

Additionally, you must have at least one non-silent partner with a liability limit to the investment amount, however, they are not involved actively in managing the partnership.

It is mandatory to file an annual tax return that details the business's earnings deducts, earnings, and loss.

But, if you are operating in a business that involves goods as an association, you could be required to submit these documents:

The annual dividend on the partnership's income.

Social security taxes are a part of employment. They include as well as Medicare contributions. Excise duty.

The partners' members On the other hand can file these documents:

Taxation on income.

Taxes for self-employment. Taxes are estimates.

Taxation on international transactions.

Partnership partners aren't considered to be employees in tax terms which is why the tax on self-employment does not apply. If you are planning to establish a brokerage for goods and you want to register a business, it might be more beneficial to do so in a partnership instead of an entity due to the favorable tax requirements. Corporations' profits as well as dividends that shareholders receive like dividends, for instance, are taxed. It is basically taxation that is double. However, this isn't the case for profits from partnerships.

Acquisition of other businesses or assets

Before deciding to sell make sure you conduct a valuation of the business to assess the worth of the business. The process is similar to the method you'd follow to assess the worth of your own company prior to closing it down or selling it.

There are many methods of the appraisal of a company, so when you are deciding to try the task yourself, make sure you do thorough investigation into the ways to do it. It is recommended to hire an experienced appraisal expert for your business. If you can determine the value the business's worth, you'll be in a position determine if you are able to finance it on your own or whether it is necessary to find an additional source of financing.

Make a acquisition agreement

In order to proceed with a merger or sale it is necessary to draft an agreement for sale. The document authorizes the purchase of assets owned by a company, or shares. It is recommended to be checked by a lawyer to make sure the accuracy and full.

Include all the inventory available to be sold, and also the names of your business and their owners. Complete the necessary details about the background of the business. Find out how the business will be managed prior to closing.

Also, determine the access level every company is entitled to financial information. Keep track of any adjustments as well as broker charges as well as other conditions in the agreement.

If liabilities or assets remain unaccounted for, it may cause issues when the sale has been completed.

Transfer ownership of a business

The conditions of your contract will outline what steps you need to take for the transfer of ownership as well as the type of ownership. It is generally advised to engage an attorney to help you in this process.

Once you've concluded the merger or acquisition, according to state laws and your business's legal structure, you'll have to declare the changes in the state.

In the event that the merger results in the demise of your former firm and the creation of a new company You may be required to establish new banks, get new federal and state tax IDs, apply to obtain permits and licenses as well as take the necessary steps to legally shut down your old company.

conducting market research and designing innovative products or services

To stay at the top of their game companies often rely on market research to help with innovative product design.

Though the process is lengthy and laborious, the new solutions and products allow companies to increase and expand their share in the market.

On average 33% of all new products do not work and never made available for sale. This is why making the investment in research for new products is crucial.

This guarantees that the effort, time and effort put into the creation of a new product idea are worth it.

Further research on product development is discussed in this piece, including what, when and the reasons to conduct it.

What is the reason to conduct Research and Product Development Market research is crucial to the development of any product in the development procedure. Why?

The software helps the owners comprehend the advantages and disadvantages of their product, and to identify the areas that need improvements.

Thus conducting market research prior to as well as during and after the development of a new product is essential to the development of any new idea.

These are the main benefits of market research in developing new products:

Customers' preferences, desires as well as needs are given priority.

Make sure you focus on areas that need improvement.

Determines market demand

Aids in pricing strategies

Develops marketing campaigns that are using data.

Make sure that the product is in line with buyer demands It also provides an excellent return on investment

Types of Product Research Methods

Research into market research to help with the development of new products can come in many forms.

The methodology of research used to conduct each study is determined by a variety of factors, including:

The goals of the project

Type of item or service

Demographics of the target audience

Schedule and timetable

However, the latest research on products typically comprises the two types of research: qualitative (statistically trustworthy) as well as qualitative research (which gives specific feedback).

Options for Quantitative Research in New Product Development

Companies looking to determine the popularity of a brand new idea Our market research company often suggests an online survey to aid in surveying data.

Online surveys that can be taken on smartphones and are usually sent out to the participants by an email.

This type of popular market research aims to gather what is the "big picture" of a undertaking.

These are just a few positive aspects that online surveys can bring to the research of new products:

They're very accessible. Surveys online are usually sent via email or specific Facebook advertisements, which makes it easy to take them using desktop, mobile tablets, and desktops.

Rapid quick response. Online surveys, regardless of whether they are B2B or C2C, are able to rapidly provide data from the target audience.

Cost-effective. This method is less expensive when compared with other methods of quantitative analysis, such as telephone or mail surveys.

Qualitative Research Options for New Product Development

There are many research studies that are available to product designers, Drive Research frequently recommends focus groups as our favorite technique.

Focus groups, in contrast individuals or IDIs can be particularly useful in gathering consensus around a particular product, service or subject.

They're particularly helpful for aiding your team to develop hypothesis, asking questions and absorbing the concepts.

Choose a business who specializes in qualitative hiring services when you want to hold focus groups as part of design research.

The participants who participate in your discussion group are specifically specific and competent.

Five benefits of focus groups that shouldn't be missed in the development of new products.

Explore more than qualitative data.

Focus groups are conceived for explorative purposes. They provide a adaptable and flexible method to gather information from consumers which does not need surveys.

Focus groups possess the distinct benefit of helping your team to gain useful, practical insights into your product or service.

Imagine that you conducted a study and found the fact that 75% of potential clients rely on reviews before making a purchase on a new product.

The focus group can go deeper to your "what" and "why?" through a focus group.

Which review websites do your customers utilize to discover products similar to ones like yours?

What is a positive score? 3 stars or higher and possibly more?

What's the value of reviews on the internet?

Take a wide range of views simultaneously.

It can take a lot of time to complete surveys. Most often, you mail the questionnaire to hundreds perhaps thousands, of respondents and have to wait for weeks before you get enough replies.

Based on the type of target public is and how many responses you'd like to get This process could be shorter or a bit longer.

Focus groups On the other hand usually consists of four to twelve people that are the closest to the buyer you want to target for your new service or product.

Participants participate in the group for a 60-90 minute conversation led by a moderator, who explains all you require to know within a flash.

Create an environment that is interactive.

Personal interaction with friends and family is always positive.

Businesses prefer face-to-face interviews in lieu of video interviews due to a reason. You can't get similar feedback online.

It's the same in comparing focus groups with surveys, particularly in the case of evaluating your idea for a product.

Chapter 5: Maintaining Your Llc

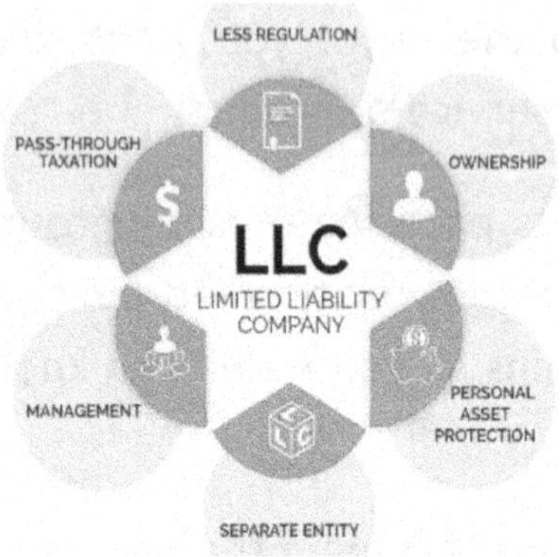

It is essential to properly manage your limited liability business following the receipt of a Certificate of Organisation from Secretary of State as well as an EIN for Federal from the IRS (LLC). If you fail to maintain your LLC properly, it LLC could result in personal liability arising from the actions of the LLC and its debts. In the event of this, you will not be able utilize the LLC's assets protection features.

In the case of receipts for expenses, deductions that you would like to be granted as well as the business's assets, proper recording is vital (what you purchased, the amount you paid for, and the depreciation). It is also important to avoid mixing the funds of business profits to purchase personal goods and reverse. Inability to maintain accurate and distinct accounting records could let a debtor "pierce the corporate veil." The phrase suggests that the protection offered by the LLC is no longer enough to protect the personal assets of your clients.

Personal liability usually is restricted to the amount that an individual has personally has invested, however the doctrine of alter ego permits the waiver of liability. In this situation the court holds individuals members accountable for debts of the corporation.

To stay clear of these practices avoid them, you should:

1. If necessary, you should file an individual tax return.

2. Complete all paperwork under the name for the LLC.

3. Maintain meticulous records

4. Meet all annual reporting required.

5. Make sure that there is enough money available for the LLC

Separate bank accounts.

A common belief is that an LLC can always protect you from personal responsibility, however this isn't the case. An LLC needs to be well maintained to offer the full protection you need.

In the case of properly managing your business, we suggest seeking the guidance of a business lawyer.

The renewal of your LLC's registration and licensing

The precise licenses and permits you need for your company will differ according to your location and business, but it's your responsibility to determine which permits and licences you require, make sure you've got them, and ensure they are up-to current.

If you do not have legal and current licenses and permits in place, you run the risk of being denied your LLC status and face penalties and even criminal charges. So don't begin working before you've got everything set up!

The operating agreement should be updated as well as other legal documents

Certain states, however not all requires LLCs to be registered under an operating agreement. Regardless of regardless of whether it's required in any way, having one is still a sensible choice, especially in the case of doing business in conjunction with more than one person.

A operating agreement outlines the responsibilities of each member, what they contributed to the company and how ownership structure is set as well as how the money is allocated and raised, when you'll add or remove members at any time, as well as when your business is dissolution.

It serves three essential tasks:

It allows you to clarify and document the verbal agreements you have with your co-partners, thus preventing any from future confusions

It allows you to establish your personal guidelines.

This protects your business's restricted liability status, by proving the fact that your company is functioning as an LLC and instead of a sole proprietorship, or partnership.

As your operating agreement will be legal and binding having a lawyer draft it is a smart decision.

Protecting your intellectual property

If you've only just created your LLC it won't be legally required to submit an annual report until at least an entire year. However, now is the best time to add it to the calendar.

The majority of states require LLCs to submit an annual report which is also known as a statement of Information (SOI). Certain states will only have to file your SOI every two years. Likewise, when you're registered with Pennsylvania there's a chance that you'll be required to file only once every 10 years.

The report you submit, whether it is annually or not, must be submitted to the Secretary of State. The majority of states allow you to complete the process online, however costs and specifications vary from state to state. A few states send reminders prior to when the due date however it's your responsibility to make sure you file it. If you do not adhere to your deadlines, you might be charged a late penalty.

If you're not in time and you are not in compliance, your LLC might be dissolution automatically.

If you've hired a business to establish your LLC and you want to know if they'll file your reports on your behalf (and the amount they cost) or whether you'll need to complete the filing yourself. Whatever the case, while you're contemplating the issue, determine when the next one is due, and then mark that date in your calendar to make sure the report is filed in the right date.

The report may seem official and daunting, but the annual report you submit isn't an email to shareholders that details what your company did during the year. The purpose of it is to verify or revise your following information:

Your principal location of commercial

Your members as well as managers' names, addresses and email addresses.

Business identification numbers are crucial like your state entity numbers

The purpose of your business

An inventory of the people who are authorized to sign

Details regarding the registered agent of your

Don't stress about it, just do it!

Maintain Detailed Records--and Keep Them Where You Can Find Them

Also, keeping minute books and other business records isn't mandatory by law, but it's a great option to ensure your safety.

Keep in mind that in case of bankruptcy, lawsuits or any other circumstance where your business's assets are in danger You must be able to prove that the LLC is distinct in relation to you as a person, proving that it's actually a business, and not merely a loophole for tax purposes. A regular record-keeping practice helps protect your personal liability in case of a lawsuit, by showing how you run your business as a legitimate business.

Complete, detailed financial records will help you cope tax issues and may be necessary if ever you require the funds to finance your company.

Keep copies of these documents in your office or work, and also backups to the cloud to be able to access the documents quickly and conveniently:

LLC Operating Agreement LLC Articles of incorporation

A confirmation letter for EIN, meeting minutes and other documents as stipulated in the operating agreement listing of all members in your LLC and the addresses of their homes, their contributions, and shares

Each financial statement, as well as the tax return

Commercial licenses, permits and licences are required.

Get Your DBA

If you've established your LLC and want to conduct business under a different title then you need to submit the form of a "doing business as" (DBA) which is also referred to as"a "fictitious name."

In this case, for instance Agnes Johnson Media LLC's proprietor might prefer doing business by registering the business as "Blissful Wedding Photography." But if she runs the business in the name, without having registered as the designation of a DBA the possibility is that she will have their LLC dissolved.

The good news is that the process of registration of the designation of a DBA is typically a straightforward and cost-effective procedure. It is not the same for every situation however, in the majority of situations, the government agency that you established the LLC will inform you of the procedures you'll need to follow. Be aware that you'll have keep your DBAs regularly (usually every year).

DBAs are also a way to manage multiple companies without having to form a new LLC. Agnes Johnson, for example is able to start "Blissful Wedding Cakes" and "Blissful Flower Arrangements" companies just by registering additional DBAs in the event she was able to obtain permissions and licences.

Liability and risk management

If you have property, like an apartment rental You may have thought about setting up an LLC to control liability. That is, becoming insurance-free. The idea is to hold those funds that normally be used for premiums on insurance. The LLC minimizes the risk you face in a lawsuit.

Tired of Paying Insurance Premiums

The cost of insurance is a concern that is a major expense for REIs (real property investors). To safeguard their LLC from liability that could arise out of the event from accidents, the vast most business proprietors utilize protection from liability insurance. Insurance firms have a track record of taking on risks and possess litigation knowledge.

While insurance may not be expensive, it's more affordable than other type of security. We believe that this strategy of not having insurance is not logical. Although insurance premiums are can be directly absorbed into profit the coverage itself is cheaper than one slip and fall.

A Properly Set Up LLC Needs Insurance

Even though a correctly formed and properly maintained LLC will safeguard your personal assets, it's not an alternative for insurance on liability. In the event of a claim for liability the majority of insurance policies give both you and your LLC with an attorney. This defense by a lawyer who is paid for much more valuable than the fees you are required to pay.

Chapter 6: Closing Your Llc

For the purpose of closing an LLC in order to close it, members have to give up the organization's capability to conduct commercial activities. This can be done by filing a complete list of Articles of Dissolution to the Secretary of State. The filing of these dissolution documents is only one aspect of dissolving a limited-liability firm. The LLC is recognized by the state in which the incorporation documents were submitted. In order to dissolve an LLC the dissolution resolution or dissolution articles as well as IRS form 966 are needed. Follow our steps-by-step procedure here and contact an UpCounsel lawyer once you're prepared.

If you don't effectively dissolve a limited liability corporation or a limited liability company, you can be subject to personal responsibility for these things:

Taxes due

Defaulted debts

Lawsuits

Limited liability businesses are required to pay a cost in a variety of states. If you don't effectively dissolve your company and you fail to do so, you could be liable to pay the cost each year. In other states, you can only be charged an amount if the restricted liability business is in operation however it has not filed an annual tax return. In the event that you fail to shut down the LLC and you fail to submit a tax return you could be penalized.

If you have property that is in the name of a limited liability corporation, you are not able to get it back up to the time that the corporation has been properly dissolved.

If you want to give up your business name and to close the permits, it is necessary to make an official LLC dissolution. Nobody will be allowed to make use of your company's name or the permits in this manner. If you make the company with limited liability in operation and do not keep an eye on it, another could use the name and cause the company legal troubles.

The dissolution of an LLC is voluntary

The Articles of Dissolution or cancellation have to be submitted to the state agency responsible for assisting with the formation of an LLC to facilitate Voluntary Dissolution. Many state agencies require all state fees and taxes to be paid in the event when the company files its article of dissolution.

The dissolution of an LLC is voluntary

In some states, remaining idle can result in being forced to dissolve an LLC because it has not complied with the requirements of the state that must be submitted annually. A procedure by when a state suspends or dissolves a charter which does not meet the requirements for filing by the state is commonly referred to as abandonment.

Divorcing your LLC and dispersing assets

If you are a Limited Liability Company has a board of directors, then the Articles of Organization usually require the approval of the board in order to dissolve the LLC. In the event that the LLC is not governed by an executive board and the primary members identified as such in the Articles of Organization may vote to dissolve the LLC or as per the guidelines stipulated in the bylaws of the LLC.

Based on the state's law as well as the conditions of the operating agreements in which the LLC is operating, some require voting on more than half of the shares in other cases, they require a unanimous vote. Consult with a tax or legal professional prior to dissolving an LLC. The first thing to check is the Buy-Sell Agreement, which establishes the regulations regarding Limited Liability Companies when they dissolve or when a LLC member chooses to quit. The Buy-Sell agreement may include relevant data for this However, if not, it is worth making one prior to proceeding with the process.

Filling out federal, state or local taxes.

Make a formal written resolution that states what the intention behind the dissolution. Have each members who voted on the dissolution to sign and date it. Then, provide a copy of the resolution to each person, since this could prove important if the legality of the dissolution later examined. The procedure to file dissolution documents Certificate of Dissolution (also known as Articles of Dissolution) varies in each state.

Some states require that you file the documents before notifying creditors and solving disputes, whereas others need to be filed after the process has been completed. Certain states need tax clearance for the company prior to submitting the Certificate of Dissolution. In such cases the business or LLC has to first pay due taxes. To find out more, you can contact Your registered agent or online incorporator or the office of Secretary of State. To ensure to ensure that your Limited Liability Company is not required to file the federal tax filing requirements File Form 966 to the IRS after 30 calendar days from the date of dissolution resolution.

All LLC permits and licences. Check about the agencies of the government that granted the LLC's permits and licenses regarding how you can end the licenses and permits. In certain instances you might be able to transfer your LLC's licences and permits to a different business structure or LLC through the formation of a new organization or LLC.

Contact tax and credit bureaus. Before LLC assets are distributed to members any known LLC obligations must be settled. Get a tax certification from the state government to prove that the LLC is current in its tax reporting requirements in the event that the state demands it.

If you want to cancel the employer Identification Number, you must contact the IRS. The IRS doesn't annul the Employer Identification Number (EIN); rather, they refer to EIN cancellation in the context of "account closure." You can cancel or remove the fake name, or DBA issued by a local or state administration. End of operation doesn't mean that tax reporting is over. obligation.

Informing creditors that your business has ended

Each creditor should be notified in writing that the firm was dissolution or submitted a declaration of intent to dissolve. The state you reside in may allow the claims of creditors who are not known in the company's name at moment of dissolution. Distribute the dissolution to:

The law in the state mandates a public announcement of dissolution in the local paper.

Write a letter to customers to inform clients that the LLC has been disbanded.

Informing creditors that the LLC intends to settle the entire balance owed, offer of settlement or filing for bankruptcy.

Settlement of claims against creditor

The liquidated company can either accept or deny claims from creditors. All accepted claims need to be paid or suitable repayment arrangements have to be reached with creditors.

All claims rejected must be communicated in written form.

Speak with a lawyer to make sure that creditor affected by the impending dissolution are notified prior to. Creditors are required to file their claims within the deadline, which varies according to the law of your state.

Transfer of remaining assets

In the event of a payment for claims and outstanding assets, they can be dispersed to owners of businesses according to the amount of the stake they hold in their business. In order to be able to distribute the assets, Internal Revenue Service must be notified of any distributions. If you have multiple classes of stock, the corporate bylaws typically describe how assets are distributed to shareholders.

Speak with your tax advisor or accountant for further information about distribution as well as your continuing future obligations. In addition, you must adhere to the state's law to the bylaws for the Limited Liability Company and distribute the LLC assets fairly for everyone members.

Final Filing of Articles

In the event of a dissolution, you must file an Articles of Dissolution or your state's equivalent at the Secretary of State in the state from which it was that the Limited Liability Company was formed with the company's name, along with the address of the LLC as well as the date of dissolution, as well as the main reason behind the dissolution. The Secretary of State's website, most states offer an online application. There will be a fee for filing. Articles of Dissolution will require a minimal filing cost. Complete and send the LLC's tax return for the final time to the IRS and tax authorities of the state. Filing the documents and articles along with other documents with the Secretary of State for your state, or with the corporation division.

Settlement of debts and other liabilities

If you are a business owner as a business owner, you are required to dissolve your LLC correctly, but in a professional manner. According the website UpCounsel the process of dissolving your business in a professional manner means paying off as much of your debts related to business that are financially viable prior to the process of dissolving. However, what happens if you are out of funds and be in debt from your business?

Liquidation of assets and the liquidation of inventory

There are a variety of events that must take place when deciding to dissolve the LLC in the event of financial difficulties. Included in this are liquidation of the company's inventory as well as assets.

The creditor is able to collect the payment from the assets of an LLC since it's separate from the owners of it. Once you have filed the paperwork for dissolving your LLC then you have to take inventory liquidation and repay creditors in order of priority. If liquidation fails to result in sufficient cash then you may use the rest of the assets to pay off any outstanding debts.

Prior to distributing the business's assets of the company among owners, first give them over to the right individuals. They can pursue you for personal damages in the event that you or any other owners hold any assets to yourself prior to trying to settle the outstanding debts.

If your circumstances are such that you are unable to keep your promises regardless of how inventive you come up with, your creditors might have to notify you that they are unable to take the debt away from the company. In extreme cases the company could be forced to declare bankruptcy for your business.

Personal responsibility for company obligations

Since LLCs are formed in the manner they have been created, creditors can't typically sue the members of LLCs individually. But, that's not always the case.

If you obtained a commercial credit with a personal assurance the loan is now the property of your personal. In the event of a default, the lender could pursue you individually to recover the loan.

Additionally, if you shut down the business prior to paying for sales tax, payroll taxes or any other tax these taxes will not go away. Federal and state agencies could personally sue you, as well as others who own the business for restitution. In addition, if you often combine your personal and professional financial affairs, creditors could pursue you for damages based on that you used your company to conceal your personal affairs.

Final tax returns are filed and other tax returns

As governments possess exceptional legal power to collect tax backs and tax liabilities, they are the most significant debts you must pay off when you are out of your business. In addition, even if you run a business as a corporation or LLC, you're personally accountable for tax liabilities like payroll taxes. Before you pay for even a single trade creditor be sure that you've complied with the tax requirements of all your employees as discussed here.

Payroll Taxes and Sales Tax

The first step is to take your final pay tax payments and submit your final employment tax forms on time in the event that you have employees. The first priority should be given to federal taxes that are withheld from the paychecks of employees, such as income tax withholding and Social Security and Medicare taxes. Taxes on state income withholding and sales tax that you've collected are next. (When filing your final tax returns include the word FINAL at the top of the tax return.) After these important tax obligations have been accomplished, you're now ready to pay for the employer's portion for Social Security and Medicare taxes. Read our post on the importance of prioritizing the repayment of business debt to find out more.

Final Income Tax Returns

If you decide to close your company, you have to adhere to a variety of IRS regulations; similarly, state regulations apply. Since tax regulations can become complex, it is worth engaging a tax consultant in particular if your firm is earning more than $50,000 per year or has several owners.

They are sole owners. You must declare your earnings and expenses and the gains and losses in Schedule C of your 1040 form as normal. Make your tax return due by April 15 of the calendar year that follows the year the business was closed. In Schedule C, there isn't a "final return" box to mark.

Limited liability companies and partnerships (LLCs). Complete Form 1065, U.S. Partnership Income Return Mark the box that states it is your last return. Complete the Form 1065 (Schedule K-1) Part of the Partner's Share of Profit, Credits deductions, etc. to declare any gains or losses that are allocated to every partner during the entire year. This form is due on or before 15th of the third month after the close of your tax year.

Corporations that have the letters C. The Form 1120 U.S. Corporation Income Tax Return is required by C corporations. Additionally, you must mark the box to indicate that this is their last tax return. This tax return must be filed prior to the 15th of the month that follows the end of firm's operations. In order to report the dissolution of their business companies must also submit

IRS Form 966 the Corporate Dissolution Form or Liquidation.

Companies with the alphabet S. Formula 1120, U.S. Corporate Income Tax Return must be submitted by C corporations. Additionally, you should make sure to check to indicate that this is their last tax return. Form 1120S, U.S. Corporation Income Tax Returns for the S Corporation, should be completed by S corporations. They must mark the box indicating for the last tax return. The form should be filed on or before the 15th day of the month that follows the end of company. In order to report the dissolution of their business corporate entities must submit IRS Form 966 corporate dissolution or liquidation.

Chapter 7 : Fundamentals Of Llc

The term "limited liability company" refers to a Limited Liability Company (abbreviated LLC)is an unofficial hybrid corporation model that gives us the benefits of a company and a Corporation i.e. the with limited liability. This means that the responsibility of third party does not have to be shared by each of the members of the firm. It is crucial, yet one of the advantages of this form of corporate governance is that it has the benefit that typically is associated with partnership arrangements, i.e., transparency taxes. A further advantage of LLCs is that they employ specific terminology for management distinct than the terminology used by different Companies and it's a good idea to highlight this since it is crucial to be aware of the various terms used in an LLC.

Glossary of an LLC

In terms of particular terminologies, I think it's best to begin by introducing incorporation, which means, merging with another business, and in this instance the term "Incorporate" gives way to "Organize," consequently the principal document that is used for the creation of an LLC is the Articles of Incorporation will be known as an Article of Organizationinstead.

A different change in terms concerns what's known as"the" Operating Agreement, which is the principal document that regulates interactions within the company. As such, unlike others, the method of the way members and directors are able to interact with the other members is not determined in laws, but rather by a particularly adaptable document.

Another distinction in terminology relates to members that are not identified as "Shareholders" or "Shareholders" however they are "Members," consequently, corporate shares aren't referred to as "Shares" or "Shares" however they are called "Membership Interest." The state of the state we establish an LLC The terminology may differ slightly between the fifty U.S. states, however the above terms are a good way to refer to a pass-partout across the various states that belong to the U.S.

How and when LLCs came into existence

The LLC was founded in 1977. However, to discover the first time in the history of business, we must be patient for nearly 20 years. In actual fact, the original Limited Liability Company was not established until the year the year 1996. The firm that made it in the history books as the very first LLC is a reference to the title from the Hamilton Brother Oil Company, one of the oil companies that was involved in commercial relations outside of the US.

The company's famed name was created by an LLC at the request of accountants, who were responsible for the risk assessment of the business; while there existed already extensively utilized types of corporations within America (C-corp as well as S-corp over all) however, the Hamilton Brothers Oil Company's accountants could not recognize in the earlier kinds of corporations what was at the time, in fact, the advantages of LLCs. They had a the ability to limit liability as well as security for avoidance of double taxation. It was a typical scenario; in essence, the base tax was initially taxed after which dividends were taxed on every shareholder.

Thus, the accountants who were having proposed the legislation that created LLCs, and to Alaska, after Alaska and having twice been denied they presented this bill in the state of Wyoming and it received unanimous approval, which led to the creation of LLCs.

LLC Act. Though LLCs had been controlled by a corporate perspective but they did not yet be fiscally regulated, in actual fact, in the year 1980 in 1980, the U.S. IRS acted in its own manner, acknowledging only limited liability, but not transparency taxation. This meant that they taxed LLCs like similar American Company.

In a short story in a way, describing the different developments, in order to reach the recognition of tax transparency we'll have to wait until 1988. After that, after the conclusion of adiatribe which ran for several years in duration, it was decided that the U.S. IRS had to accept the transparency tax. For us to reach Limited Liability Companies as we are today, we would need to wait an additional eight years after, upon the request of a few New York lawyers some of LLCs' flaws could not get rid of were eliminated.

One of the greatest benefits of an LLC is that it can choose the "Tax Regime," that means, based on my personal preference, Ican decide to elect the LLC to be a"C-CORP" instead of being an "S-CORP." The second advantage lies in the creation of "the operating agreement" i.e. the document that regulates the relationships among the partners as well as between directors.

The most significant feature i.e. the possibility to share remuneration for earnings in a non-proportional fashion, i.e., if there are more than two members, it's possible to make sure that their share in the loss and profits is not proportional to the shareholding of each partner and, therefore, to the number of"Share Shares" or "Share Shares" the respective owners have in the LLC.

The Role of Partners

One could argue, in this case that an LLC gives its members - the owners- the members- the ability to divide profits however they like and equate them to self-employed employees, while taxing the same as self-employed workers and, when a member of a Limited Liability firm, the entire body will dissolve, and remaining members are able to decide whether or not to create a new LLC. In particular, members of an LLC can be protected from individual freedom in the event of company debts as well as possible claims such as if the business has to repay the creditor, the person or organization is not able to collect that obligation directly from the members or take over personal assets. In a situation similar to this, are likely to be liable only for the amount they put into the company, however their participation in a personal way may be needed, in particular the following situations:

In the event that the individual member assures a loan from a bank or business loan in the event that the LLC fails to pay

if the employee does not pay taxes that are withheld from wages of employees

If he is acting illegally or in a fraudulent manner, causing damage to the business or individuals

If it uses the LLC to extend of its own business, rather than as a distinct tax and legal entity: This last aspect specifically can result in problems with the law.

Pros and Cons

After we've laid out the fundamental aspects in aLimited Liability Company (LLC), let's examine the pros and cons this business has to offer, and the situations in which it could be - or not be - the best choice for the needs of the individual. It is important to remember that an LLC isn't an positive or negative option it's all about your goals for business and how you wish to handle your affairs in addition to the ideal tax position for your members and the business as a whole, based on your business activities that you plan to conduct.

The advantages of forming an LLC within the United States are:

Limit personal liability for individuals, which has been previously mentioned. Shortly, members' personal resources do not serve as a means for the purpose of reducing liabilities, except for the specific circumstances defined.

It's generally safe for smaller businesses since it needs minimal documentation which means it is a fairly simple incorporation process. This is partly since it does not have to form, for instance the board of directors, or any other corporate committees.

Every member has the option of deciding what percentage to contribute to the gains

There are benefits to taxation too as the tax pass-through for LLCs guarantees the exact situation that all earnings and expenses are passed directly to the members of their tax taxes.

LLCs: their negatives

Be aware that, as we've stated, there aren't definitive pros or cons however, everything must be assessed in relation to the way you will run your business. We will consider what the advantages of forming an LLC could be.

An LLC will cease to exist at when a partner quits it. To remain, it must start the process of forming of a brand new business

In certain states, LLcs are considered franchise tax-exempt that can lead to hidden costs

A further hidden expense is the annual reports which must be filed. We are going to learn more on in the next article.

The summary is that, although it is an incredibly straightforward and efficient corporate model but its benefits is not to be taken for to be taken for granted. It is essential to consult an expert in the field that, after carefully considering the whole picture from both a legal and tax viewpoint can give advice to members about the ideal kind of arrangement.

LLC and Corporation: The Main Differences

A different constitution for LLCs is corporations. They are limited liability businesses where the shares of shareholders are reflected in shares. The capital stock is split into annumerary of securities each of which contains a certain shareholding, as well as rights of the corporate in that shareholding. Be aware that it is crucial to get the guidance of an expert within the field in order to determine the best option for you There are instances where it's preferable to move forward by establishing either the corporate or other structure:

If you are planning to purchase and then bringing in income for a property it's more straightforward to do this via an LLC that matches every property to an adedicated llc since depreciation for each unit will reset the tax when the year.

If the ownership of the business is already an incorporation then it is best to create a corporation to stay clear of especially high taxes, which we'll see in the future in the discussion of taxation that LLCs are subject to;

If you decide in the future to invite more investors to the company then the corporate structure is the ideal choice as it's formal, and thus more secured;

LLCs, as opposed to corporations, require members to submit tax returns to the u.s. The reason for this is that it is essential to keep this information to be considered when you evaluate every member's fiscal and legal situation.

From Single-Member LLC to Multi-Member

If you run a limited liability business by yourself, and wish to increase the number of owners, then you need to go through the process of changing the single-member LLC to one that is a Multi-member LCC (known informally as partners). The rules for the rules for an LLC are based on the state that it was formed in. The main laws, on the contrary on the other hand, apply for every state. The process of adding a new member is typically required to be outlined in the Articles of Organization that are created at the time an LLC is established. In this article we'll discuss ways to include new members to a legal manner within your state.

Operating agreement, or written consent

The procedure a person or business must complete in order to join the LLC in the event that the operating contract stipulates the conditions to be a member. If those terms don't get written down, they could be negotiated by the consent by all members. It must be inclusive of the individual or company's ownership share as well as its all-encompassing, signed and written acceptance.

Chapter 8: Get Funds From Investors

Allow employees to own a stake within the LLC.

If the operating contract does not yet outline the procedure for operations and how to proceed, you must follow the laws in the state where you reside to allow for adding members. Be sure to adhere to these guidelines if you don't wish to be accountable for your actions and are looking to avoid issues with ownership at some point in the future. Take a look at the advantages and disadvantages of adding another person of your LLC

The new owner could bring new perspectives and abilities. The amount of money that you earn will decrease.

Other opinions from a individual decision maker should be taken into account.

It could be difficult to remove the status of a partner during an unresolved dispute.

If you're unsure who is someone you'd like to conduct business with, consider how you might meet the needs that you have set for yourself and the LLC without adding another member. When a new member is accepted, their name should be included in the incorporation documents and the operating contract is required to be updated to indicate the amount of stake he is able to take. Certain states require LLCs to disband and re-form in the event that the members who control the LLC are changed. If your company has just one owner and doesn't have an operating agreement in place, it's best to draft one before the addition of a member. That's how the division of losses and profits will be written down. Over the long term this could reduce your expenses and save time.

Identifying the particulars

LLCs enjoy a dynamic ownership structure that allows members' share of ownership does not have for it to correspond to the amount of the profits they earn. The operating agreement may be modified when the majority of members have agreed to the following guidelines:

Name of newest member.

The value of the capital contribution that he has made. The percentage of the participation.

The percentage of its share of profits and its share of losses and profits.

Accept the amended agreement following accepting the change through a formal voting of the shareholders. The revised agreement should be filed with the other documents required for LLC.

Notification of authorities

A majority of states require secretary of state is informed of any modifications in the constitution in an LLC. Other states must file a list of members and their managers each year. The list can be modified as a new member joins. If your LLC automatically taxed as a pass-through entity it is necessary to choose whether you want to tax this way when you fill out IRS Form 8832 each time you are adding a member. It is due to the fact that LLCs having multiple members are considered partnerships when they are taxed by default. If you add a new participant to an LLC it is crucial to consider tax implications.

Domestic LLC vs. Foreign LLC

Domestic LLCs are those which is registered within your home state (your home state). When you create an LLC in a different state that your home state you have to register your company within your state of residence as a foreign LLC. For clarity this, the phrase "foreign" has really no connection with the company located or owned outside of the United States by anonresident of the United States. This simply means that the firm is working in a different state than its home. What's the significance of this?

In order to establish an L.L.C within a different state it is possible to create two entities: one at your state of incorporation, as well as one within the state you reside in. If you reside in Indiana however you want to form as an LLC within Wisconsin. In order to be able to operate in the state you reside in You must establish your business as an foreign LLC within Indiana. It is necessary to fill out all the steps twice if you own two LLCs. State filing fees for two states Registered agents for both states, 2 yearly reports, and many additional expenses are also comprised. The formation of two LLCs can double your expenditure and cause problems.

Also, do certain states more suitable than others to establish an LLC? Absolutely. However, for the vast most people forming an LLC in their own home state will be the ideal option. Many people read or hear any online content that says, "Nevada has no corporate income tax"and think that Nevada is the perfect state to establish an LLC. Although the first assertion may be correct but the second statement is not in all cases, and especially not those who live within Nevada. (We will discuss Nevada more in the coming weeks). Why? Keep in mind that you'll be required to create a foreign LLC within your state of residence. Therefore, you'll be required to pay tax within your state of residence and the other tax that is required for establishing two LLCs.

The notion that you could create an LLC in a"tax-free" state, but choose to be taxed as an entity and not have to pay any income taxes within your state of residence is not true at all. Many people prefer to establish their LLC within their home state. There is no way to benefit from forming an LLC in another country. In fact, the likelihood is that it'll cost you more over the course of time as well as the long term.

How to Open An LLC Step-By-Step

We've already discussed, the process of forming an LLC isn't an extremely complicated procedure. The steps to follow are listed below:

Find out the which U.S. state to open the business. Choose the name, and then look into the possibility of opening that same name.

Apply for an EIN -Employer Identification Number. This number is needed for the process of completing Form SS-4 issued by the Department of the Treasury Internal Revenue Service.

Check to see if you've established an account with a US-based bank before proceeding to the incorporation of your company.

We will look at, practical aspects of the procedures that must be followed.

Selecting a business name

It is crucial to be aware you must remember LLC name must not appear similar to that of existing businesses The best approach is and also a good idea choosing a straightforward and distinct name.In further, when selecting the name of your business it is crucial to examine the naming choice from a marketing perspective in order to convey the essence of what the business does and how it is positioned within the market. Apart from these elements essential to understand that there are specific words that cannot be used within corporate names. Specifically:

The names that indicate that the business is a government company, but not a government entity. words such as bank, city or insurance. These names suggest the work of particular professionals can't be utilized if the LLC.

Chapter 9: Tax Implications

Other important details to ensure managing the LLC.

The operating agreement is an essential document that can be used to resolve any disputes that may arise, safeguarding the rights of all members. Additionally, it's essential to understand that LLC members are able to decide they will manage their own operations by appointing a co-ordinating managing member, or decide to work with an external manager.

Costs associated with forming an LLC

The formation of an LLC requires the existence of certain fixed expenses, and these must be taken into consideration when choosing to go ahead with the formation of a company:

First, using a professional makes a difference to every aspect. So, should you are planning to establish an LLC, it's beneficial to consult a specialist.

Filing Fee is the expense of registering your business The registration fee is an enforceable necessity. The fee typically ranges from $150 to $880.

The cost for publishing of newspapers in certain states have a requirement to release in newspapers that are recognized by the government, the official notice of the incorporation date of the business in order to sets the foundation for the corporate processes. The publication should last for at least six weeks. The price can range from $1,500 to $2,500.

Annual Report : it is a fee for each year that reveals to the public that the company is actually operating the business. In general, the Annual Report is around $200 each year.

The fee for the work of the Registered Agent, an obligatory figure that is that is responsible for managing various administrative processes. Simply put, it is a representative role that is, the person in charge are responsible for handling all correspondence, which comes from and eventually must be delivered to US government officials. The cost for this position and can be either an internal or external one for the organization and is around $100 annually.

The constitution of Operating Agreement The Operating Agreement has an unassailable cost for drafting and filing the contract, which could be by hundreds of dollars.

As a summary, the expense for establishing an LLC and running it each year could be anywhere in the region between $3,000 and $4,000.It is essential to take the costs into consideration, with the addition of additional tax and legal obligations can be easily added in the event of forming the company.

How to start Your LLC in California

The LLC you create can be set up in California LLC in eight easy steps if you've determined that LLCs are an ideal company structure to meet your needs.

1. The name of your California LLC

Names must be established for your LLC before you file your Articles of Formation. The rules for naming an LLC for your LLC in California are to be observed. These guidelines must be considered above all other than:

The name of your company must include all letters Limited Liability Company, LLC or L.L.C.

The name should be distinguished from an existing company name that is being used by the state. If you want to know if a specific company name is used, look up the website of Secretary of State.

The name of the government agency can't be used as a company names (e.g., State Department, FBI, CIA, Treasury and so on.).

Certain terms that are not permitted (such like lawyer, bank, credit union, attorney etc.) may require additional documentation as well as a license.

Another thing to take into consideration the accessibility of URLs. It is essential to have a website even if you don't believe you need one. By securing your domain today will allow you to have the chance to get one at a later date. Prior to deciding on a name for your LLC look into whether your domain is available.

Place your name in the hold. If you're still not yet ready to formalize your Limited Liability Company, but need to ensure that you've got the name you're looking for, make a reservation for it at a cost. Names registered in California are available for at least 60 days, paying the cost and then submitting necessary paperwork with the state's government.

#2 Selecting an agent registered

In California the state of California, the LLC has to select an agent registered with the state.

The person or entity who is designated as your LLC's authorized agent can take service of process, along with other official legal notices and papers. Legal documents, official communications tax forms, as well as notices of legal proceedings are all sent to this individual or entity for the benefit of the LLC.

Any person or entity which provides registration services for instance, you, or an employee in your LLC is a registered agent. The registration must meet these requirements:

The services of registered agents must be provided by organizations (or companies).

Agent's address should be located in California.

During normal business hours agents must be available and on site to receive the necessary paperwork.

#3 Draft and send the incorporation articles

Articles of Organization Articles of Organization are apaper which legalizes the formation of the legal entity of your LLC and provides basic information. Articles of

Organization should be submitted with the Form LLC-1 to California.

For a proper registration of the correct registration of your California LLC, draft the Articles of Organization and submit them to the Secretary California. California. Though it could seem like a lot of work the only thing you need to do is completing and submitting an online brief form. It is possible to send it to us too. It is common to require the following information to make the item:

The name and address of the location of your LLC

The goal of the LLC.

A list of the name of your registered agent as well as the address.

Structure of the organization Will the LLC be managed by members or by managers?

The documents must be signed by the person who created the LLC.

A Secretary of State is required to review the application once the documents are filed. If the documents are approved then the LLC can be considered legitimately operating. It is possible to submit the application to California in person, via the web or via post.

Fourth, obtain a certification from the federal government.

When the LLC registration forms are filed and accepted by the state and accepted by the state, it will issue an official certificate that indicates the LLC is officially registered. One of the easiest ways to receive the certificate is through online filing.

The LLC is able to establish a business bank account and also the Employment Identification Number (EIN) and also business licenses with the assistance of this document.

#5 Draft an operational agreement

Operating agreements serve as an outline of the way your LLC is to operate.

Operating agreements are required for residents of California However, it's not required to file. The agreement should be straightforward to reach. An operating agreement in writing can assist in resolving differences over financial arrangements, and any other potential conflicts, among other issues. In the absence of a contract, state law determines the decisions of courts and could not necessarily be in the LLC's or the members the best interest. This isn't all-encompassing list of things the operating agreement might include:

Name and the primary address for the LLC. LLC

Timeframe of the LLC

The name and address that of the registered agent.. Information concerning the current status of the organisation

What is the purpose of the activity?

Members and the amount they've done to make a difference. Method of dividing earnings and losses

A procedure for taking on new members or removing current members.

Control of the LLC

The liability and indemnity clauses

#6 Submitting an abridgement of details

Within 90 days after the LLC's formation The LLC must submit a Statement of Information to the Secretary of State. California LLCs have to file a Statement of Information to the California Secretary of State. In the information statement:

The name of the LLC as well as its California Secretary of State number for filing.

Agent's name and address

Where is the major executive office?

Chapter 10: The Address For The Llc In The Form Of A Written

Each managing director or manager must be able to provide their full name, as well as the address of their home or job If no manager is selected, every individual's name as well as address.

The address of the LLC's email (if the LLC decides to get renewals via e-mail rather than regular mail)

Primary line of business used by the LLC

#7 Get an identification tax number for the employer of your

The Internal Revenue Service (IRS) provides the LLC Employer Identification Number of a single digit (EIN) to facilitate tax purposes. With the help of IRS they can seek an EIN via mail or on the internet. EINs are issued to help with: EIN will assist to address the following issues:

Filing tax returns and completing the forms at the federal and state levels.

Set up a bank account for your business.

Personnel for hiring.

8. Pay the annual franchise tax

In California an LLC that is a limited liability (LLC) is required to pay an franchise tax of $800. This tax has to be paid every year, regardless of whether or not the business has made profits in the preceding year. If the LLC's an annual revenue of more than $250,000, it will have to be liable for an additional tax amount in the amount of $10,000 each year.

The rule does not apply in the case of California Limited Liability Companies formed in 2021, 2022 or 2023. In accordance with the law change the California limited liability corporation who files for registration of business or the formation of a company is not required to pay the franchise tax at a minimum of $800 during its first fiscal year of taxation. The following year of taxation the LLC has to pay the tax of $800.

How to start Your LLC in Florida

#1: Provide your LLC aFlorida name.

It is essential to choose a name for your LLC prior to filing your Articles of Formation. Names must be in line with the Florida naming rules. These guidelines must be considered above all other criteria:

The words Limited Liability Company, LLC or L.L.C. must be used in the name.

The business name should be distinctive in comparison to other similar businesses within the state. To determine if a particular company name is being used, look up the Secretary of State's site. Go to this website to discover the availability of a particular name within Florida.

The name of the government agency can't be used as a company names (e.g., Department of State, CIA, FBI, Treasury, etc.).

Certain restricted terms (such like lawyer, bank attorney, credit union etc.) might require additional documents as well as a license.

Check out the Florida regulation on naming to the fullest extent.

Another thing to take into consideration URL accessibility. If you're not convinced you'll need a web site it is likely that you'll need. At the very least, purchase the domain name you want now in order so that you have the possibility to have one in the future. Make sure your URL is accessible prior to making a decision on the name for your LLC.

Place your name in the hold. If you're still not in the process of registering your LLC but you're concerned your name may already be used then you can secure the name by paying a nominal fee. Names are not reserved within Florida.

#2 Select an approved agency.

Florida is a law that requires the LLC pick a registered agent. As a representative of the LLC services of process as well as other legal papers and notifications can be sent at the address of the registered agent. The registered agent could be a private individual (such as yourself or a representative of the LLC)or an entity that is an agent registered with the government. The registered agent must adhere to these requirements:

The services of registered agents must be provided by organizations (or companies).

The address of the agent's residence has to reside in Florida.

In normal hours of business agents must be present and available to receive documents.

3. Draft and reserve the articles of incorporation

The articles of incorporation provide the LLC's essential requirements and formal create the entity. The articles of organization must be written and send these to Florida Division of Corporations for approval in the event that you want to legally establish your LLC within Florida. While it might seem difficult the only thing you need to do is to fill in and submit an online brief form. It is possible to send it to us also. The most common information to make the item:

Name, address and principal location for the principal location of business for the LLC. The name of your registered agent and address (post offices won't be considered acceptable).

The full addresses and names that are provided by each LLC's members. If the LLC is owned by partners, the managers name as well as the address.

the reason behind the foundation of your LLC. It can be interpreted as the generalization.

how long the LLC the length of time it will exist. They are usually permanent. This means that they will have an indefinite time frame. They can be dissolvable at any time or involuntarily dissolve an LLC. It is necessary to provide the expiration date of the purpose for which your LLC was created when it is a fixed end date.

The organization structure of the LLC will be managed by the its management or members?

The documents have to be signed by the owner that creates the LLC. In Florida the registered agent too is obligatory to sign the articles.

The secretary of state is required to review the paperwork once the articles have been submitted. If the article is accepted and accepted, the LLC can be considered legitimate business.

4. Get a certificate from the federal government.

Once the LLC form forms are received and deemed acceptable and accepted by the state, it will issue an official certificate that indicates the LLC has now been registered. The LLC will then be able to establish a business bank account and the employment ID number (EIN) as well as business licenses with the assistance of this document.

#5 Draft an operationalized contract

An operating agreement is a guideline for the way the LLC operates. While Florida doesn't require that the LLC have an operating agreement but it's a crucial aspect of running your business. There are a myriad of reasons, like settlement of disagreements concerning financial arrangements or potential lawsuits, having a legally-drafted and accessible operating agreement is beneficial. In the absence of a contract, state law determines court decisions and might not necessarily be in the company's or the members the best interest. It is not an exhaustive list of the contents an operating agreement might comprise:

Name and the primary address for the LLC. LLC

The name and address of LLC's members

Timeframe of the LLC

Contact details for the agent registered

Details on the Articles of Incorporation

Goal of the Company

Members and how they've done to help

involvement in the company including voting rights and participation in the business, voting privileges, and.

Losses and profits distribution agreements Procedures for being a member and departing. Control of the LLC's conditions of dissolution and indemnity clauses

#6 Applying for an employment ID number.

The Internal Revenue Service (IRS) provides the LLC an Employer Identification Number of digits (EIN) for tax purposes. With the help of IRS you can get your EIN through post or on the internet. The purpose of an EIN can aid you with:

Tax filing for federal and state taxes and management.

Chapter 11: How Do You Start The Llc In Texas?

1. Make sure you give the Texas LLC aname

It is necessary to choose a name for your LLC before you file your documents of incorporation. Names must be in line with Texas regulations on naming. These guidelines must be considered above all other criteria:

The term Limited Liability Company, LLC or L.L.C. should be included in the business' name.

Names must be distinctive in comparison to other similar businesses that are in the same state. To determine if a particular company name is used, search on the website of Secretary of State. Check this site to find out the availability of a particular name within Texas.

The name of a government agency cannot be used as a company names (e.g., State Department, CIA, FBI, Treasury and so on.).

Certain restricted terms (such such as lawyer, bank, credit union, attorney etc.) may require additional documentation and a license.

Other things to consider:

Availability of URLs. If you don't have a site it is likely that you should. At minimum, register your domain name as soon as possible in order to have the option of getting one at a later date. Verify if your URL is accessible prior to making a decision on the name for your LLC.

Place your name in the hold. If you're not ready to create your LLC however you are worried that the name you're looking for might already be used You can reserve the name with a small fee. After paying the fee and then submitting the appropriate paperwork to the authorities of the state the names of Texas may be reserved for at least 120 days.

#2 Selecting a registered agent

Texas requires the LLC pick a registered agent. Registered agent refers to the entity or entity chosen by the LLC to be notified of other legal documents as well as notifications. The registered agent could be a person (such as you, or the representative of the LLC) or a company which provides services to registered agents. They must comply with these requirements:

The services of registered agents must be provided by organizations (or firms).

The residence of the agent must reside in Texas.

In normal hours of business agents must be available and on site to sign the necessary paperwork.

#3 Type the Certificate of Formation, and return it.

A Certificate of Formation, also called the Articles of Organization in other states, is a document which officially establishes your LLC and provides you with access to important details. In order to legally register the legal entity of your LLC in Texas create a Certificate of Formation. Then, you must send this to the Texas Secretary of State. While it might seem to be a bit difficult, the only thing necessary is to fill in and submit a brief online application. It is possible to mail it to us too. The most common information to make an incorporation certificate

The name of your LLC (including your name).

An inventory of your registered agent's name as well as address.

What was the reason for you to establish the LLC. This could be a generalization.

how long the LLC is in existence. They are usually permanent, meaning they are able to have an unlimited time frame. They can be dissolvable at any time or involuntarily dissolve an LLC. It is necessary to provide the expiration date for your LLC's mission in the event that it is a fixed end date.

The organization structure of the LLC will be managed by members or management? members?

The address and name of every founding partner, If the LLC is operated by the partners.

Name and address of the manager who was the first to be named If the LLC is managed by managers.

The name and address of the founder of the LLC.

the date that certifications begin.

The certificate must be signed by the individual who created the LLC.

A Secretary of State will review the Certificate of Formation when it has been filed. In the event that the Certification of Formation gets approved and accepted, the LLC can be considered to be legitimate business.

Fourth, obtain a certification from the federal government.

Once the LLC's documents for formation has been received and approved and accepted, the State can issue a certificate to confirm the official status of your LLC. The LLC can create a business bank account as well as an employee ID number (EIN) as well as permit for business with the aid of this document.

#5 Draft an operational agreement

Operating agreements serve as an outline of the way the LLC operates. While filing an operating agreement isn't required to be filed in Texas for LLCs, it's a crucial aspect of running your business. Due to a range of reasons, like the resolution of disputes that may arise concerning financial arrangements or legal proceedings, having a written and accessible operating agreement is beneficial. In the absence of a contract, state law regulates the decisions of courts and might not be in the best interests of the LLC or the members the best interest. This isn't an exhaustive list of the contents the operating agreement might comprise:

The name and principal location of the LLC. LLC

Timeframe of the LLC

The certificate of incorporation, which includes the name of the registered agent as well as address

The contributions of the members as well as the objectives of the organisation. splitting losses and gains

The procedure for welcoming new members as well as removing existing members

Control of the LLC

Indemnity and liability clauses

#6 Applying for an employment identification number

The Internal Revenue Service (IRS) gives the LLC Employer Identification Number (EIN) for tax purposes. With the help of IRS it is possible to seek an EIN through mail or via the web. The purpose of an EIN will assist in the following areas:

Filing tax returns and completing the forms both at federal and astate levels.

Open a bank account on behalf of your business.

Personnel for hiring.

#7 Submitting aPublic Information Report and LLC Franchise Tax.

The Texas Comptroller's Office requires all LLCs in Texas to file an annual Franchise Tax as well as a Public Information Report. Franchise Tax as well as Public Information Reports for your LLC should be filed annually on or before the 15th of May. First reports are not needed until one year following the creation in the LLC.

How do you begin an LLC in Georgia

The name of Your Georgia LLC is.

It is necessary to choose a name for your LLC prior to filing the documents of incorporation. Names must be in line with Georgia's name guidelines. These guidelines should be considered above all other criteria:

LLC, L.L.C. (or Limited Liability Company, must include the word "Limited Liability Company" in the company's name.

Names must be distinctive when compared with other businesses that are operating in the state. To determine if a particular company name is being used, look up the Secretary of State's site. Go to this website to discover whether a name is already available for sale in Georgia.

A name from a government entity is not able to be used in the corporate trademark (e.g., State Department, CIA, FBI, Treasury and so on.).

Certain terms that are not permitted (such such as lawyer, bank attorney, credit union etc.) may require additional documentation and a license.

Check out the Georgia regulation on naming complete.

Another thing to take into consideration URL accessibility. Although you may not think that you need a website but you will likely need one. It is recommended that you at the very least, purchase the domain name you want now in order so that you have the possibility of having it later. Make sure your URL is accessible prior to making a decision on the name for your LLC.

You can put your name off. If you're still not ready to create your LLC however you are worried that the name you'd like might already be used or reserved, you can make a nominal payment. Names can be secured in Georgia through the payment of money and submitting the appropriate application to state officials for a period of up to 30 days.

#2 Choose an agent registered with the government.

Georgia requires that the LLC select a registered agent. As a representative of the LLC the service of process as well as other official legal papers and documents can be sent directly to the agent registered. The registered agent can be a person (such as you, or an agent of the LLC) as well as a corporation which provides services to registered agents. The registered agent must comply with these requirements:

The services of registered agents must be made available by businesses (or companies).

The residence of the agent must be located in Georgia.

During office hours during the day The agent should be available and present to collect the necessary documents.

#3 Draft, and Save the Articles of Incorporation

Articles of incorporation is a document that officially establishes your LLC in order to outline its essential specifics. For legal registration of your LLC create the documents of organization and then submit your documents to Corporations Division of the Georgia Secretary of State. While it might seem difficult the only thing you need to do is fill in and submit an online brief form. It is possible to mail it too. It is necessary for preparing your documents to mail:

The name of your LLC

The person filling out the form must also the person who filled it out must. An administrator, a partner, LLC attorney, or any other person who is organizing the paperwork can be mentioned as an organizer.

Complete this Transmittal Informational Georgia LLC form to create articles online. It must include the following information on the form:

Email address for the LLC's mailing

Chapter 12: The Principal Office Of The Llc's Post Office Box

LLC's name, as well as the reservation code for the name (if there is one)

Name and address of the person who filed the documents and the registered agent's name as well as the address of the address and names.

The secretary of state is required to review the application once the documents are filed. If the documents are approved and accepted, the LLC can be considered legitimate business.

Fourth, obtain a certification from the federal government.

The business officially begins after the Secretary of State accepts your articles of incorporation. A Secretary of State can review the form and send you a certificate of incorporation to your company address within five to seven business days. The LLC will be able to establish a business bank account and also the employment ID number (EIN) as well as permit for business purposes with the aid of this document.

#5 Draft an operational agreement

Operating agreements serve as a blueprint for how the LLC is to operate. A written operating agreement is essential for any business, regardless of whether the state you are in mandates for it or otherwise. There are many reasons to have an operating agreement such as settling disputes that may arise over the financial arrangement and other potential litigation, having a properly documented and accessible operating agreement is beneficial. Without a formal contract, the states' laws govern the decisions taken by courts that could not be in the best interests of the LLC or the members the best interest. This isn't a complete listing of the terms that an operating agreement might contain.

Name and the primary address for the LLC. LLC

Timeframe of the LLC

The name and address for the agent registered with the organization.. Details about the state of the organisation

What is the purpose of the activity?

Members and how they've made available

A method of splitting profits and losses

A procedure for welcoming new members as well as removing existing members.

Control of the LLC

The liability and indemnification clauses

#6 Applying for an employment ID number.

The Internal Revenue Service (IRS) gives the LLC Employer Identification Number of a single digit (EIN) for tax purposes. With the help of IRS they can seek an EIN via mail or on the internet. EINs are issued to help with: EIN will assist to address the following issues:

Filing tax returns and completing the forms both at federal and asstate levels.

Set up a bank account for your business.

Personnel for hiring.

What to do when you want to convert your business into an LLCThere are many benefits of converting to the LLC structure if you already are a company, specifically when it's an sole proprietorship or a general partnership. Sole proprietorships and general partnership are not equipped with this feature, making the company an entirely different legal entity when you create an LLC. Personal assets are protected from litigation if your company gets sued, since you're the legal entity you own.

1. Start a brand new LLC business entity and then incorporate it. No matter if you're beginning a new business or operating an existing one, the procedure is identical. In this case, for instance, you could make an online

application to the office of Secretary of State in Texas.

2. Make an application to obtain a brand new Employer Identification Number through the Federal Government (EIN). The LLC that is created LLC will require its own identification number since it's an entirely separate entity from the former company structure.

3. Stop any bank accounts which were established under the name of the former company structure. Transfer funds into new accounts set up by the LLC's name, and using an EIN.

4. Assign the new business owner the ownership of all machines, real estate and assets, as well as licenses and permits. This could include real estate, equipment, as well as cars. There is no more apprehension in any dispute about these assets when the LLC owns the assets. As an example it is the LLC is not responsible for any damages if the LLC is responsible for damage if someone gets injured while on your premises of work and

your property is registered under the name of the LLC. This means that it is not possible to liquidate your personal property like your home, in order to pay a claim.

5. Modify insurance contracts in order to ensure that the LLC will be covered should a claim arise.

6. Inform your vendors and clients inform them that you've changed your company structure. Contracts might need be amended or brand they may need to be drafted in order in order to reflect the newly formed LLC business, based on the particular ties.

What happens when an LLC shut down?

In general, LLCs are separated when it becomes insolvent, when one partner leaves and it is required to be rebuilt, or internal problems develop or management issues arise or the company is not able to meet its working capital requirements. What steps are required to approve dissolution generally include:

The decision to dissolve the business has to be approved by the company's members and a certificate of dissolution

The tax authorities should be informed of the tax authorities with proper documentation in addition to the salary of employees who are not paid are to be paid. In addition, creditors should be informed of the need to make formal the claims.

If you are reaching out to creditors, it's important to also include the deadline by when a claim can be made after that date it will not be permitted.

Capital and assets are to be divided in accordance with the equity share of members

The dissolution papers must be submitted to the appropriate authorities. This action will then result in the dissolution of the business.

As we've observed, although this is by far the most straightforward type of company found in the United States the process of forming and operating an LLC still requires an understanding of tax law. It is true that the u.s. Irs is famous as being among the "Lightest" In the world however, it's also widely known that tax audits are common and that the margins of error in the event of violations are nearly negligible.

Tax Benefits

It is important to consider the benefits and costs of various legal structures that you can use for your business, starting with the way they impact your tax liability and also the protection of the personal assets you own. Limited liability companies are the ideal choice for the situation.

The proprietors of a limited liability entity are not personal liable for financial obligations or conduct of the firm, in contrast to partnerships or sole proprietorships. LLCs are now becoming more popular lieu of Cand Scorporations for the tax advantages, greater flexibility, and less administration burden.

For taxation purposes in terms of taxation LLC can be a viable for a business structure you can think about. If you're seeking a way to reduce and simplify the federal income tax returns An LLC could be the right choice for you. Additionally, you won't be at risk of liability for personal responsibility or the loss of personal assets. But it is essential to examine your goals and decide whether forming a limited liability company is the right choice for your company. There is no need to be an absolute decision that leaves no room for discussion. LLCs are particularly adaptable when it comes to restructuring in the future and this is crucial because your needs are bound to change in the course of time.

Make sure you read the state's laws and consult with your accountant in the course of your research. Be sure to review the business's continuity plan in order to be prepared to handle any eventuality. Are you of the opinion that LLC is the most suitable company structure for you as well as other entrepreneurs because of its tax advantages and cost it can save for the business? Consider both its benefits as well as the drawbacks.

There are many advantages to forming an LLC

1. Pass-through taxation.

The ability to avoid double taxation is a major advantage of having an LLC. They are "pass-through entities." According to the IRS. In the eyes of the IRS, LLC members are not required to pay corporation income tax in the eyes of the federal government. Owners can instead opt to include their own portion of their business's earnings or losses in their own personal tax return. The name suggests that "pass-through taxation," avoids double taxation, by shielding companies from tax liability at the personal and corporate and individual levels.

2. Select the tax method you want to pay.

the freedom to pick one's tax method is perhaps the biggest advantage of having an LLC. The limited liability company (LLC) may choose to tax in the form of a partnership, sole proprietorship or corporation and partnerships. Your LLC's earnings will be treated in the same way as your personal earnings when you file your tax returns regardless of whether or not you decide to be taxed as sole proprietorship or as a corporation.

The income of your LLC is taxed twice when you decide to operate as a corporation, first at an individual level, as well as in the corporation level however, at a reduced rate for the first $75,000 portion of your earnings. Based on your individual expenditure habits and plans to invest in your business either strategy could prove advantageous.

3. Take business expenses off.

The development of a new startup process could be extremely costly. There's good news, many of the costs can be tax-deductible as per the Internal Revenue Service. The way in which an LLC was formed under federal tax law the LLC's owner has the right to claim the cost to get the company established. The expenses incurred by the proprietor of an LLC at the beginning stages of development for business are deemed to be start-up expenses and therefore tax-deductible. Marketing, training for personnel expenses, travel, as well as anything else required in order to make the business and operating prior to the first sale falls under the category of start-up costs.

After you've officially opened your company, you'll be able to keep taking deductions for things such as Internet service, phone service, lunches for business, charges for accountancy, as well as the cost of renting an office. The following are the many kinds of tax deductions available for LLCs and corporate entities.